Subjective Realist Cinema

SUBJECTIVE REALIST CINEMA
From Expressionism to Inception

Matthew Campora

berghahn
NEW YORK • OXFORD
www.berghahnbooks.com

Published in 2014 by
Berghahn Books
www.berghahnbooks.com

© 2014 Matthew Campora

All rights reserved. Except for the quotation of short passages
for the purposes of criticism and review, no part of this book
may be reproduced in any form or by any means, electronic or
mechanical, including photocopying, recording, or any information
storage and retrieval system now known or to be invented,
without written permission of the publisher.

Library of Congress Cataloging-in-Publication Data

Campora, Matthew.
　Subjective realist cinema : from expressionism to Inception / Matthew Campora.
　　pages cm
　Includes bibliographical references and index.
　ISBN 978-1-78238-278-2 (hardback) — ISBN 978-1-78238-279-9 (institutional ebook)
　1. Motion pictures—Philosophy.　2. Subjectivity in motion pictures.　3. Realism in motion pictures.　I. Title.
　PN1995.C3415 2014
　791.43'612—dc23　　　　　　　　　　　　　　　　　　　　　　　　　　2013023314

British Library Cataloguing in Publication Data

A catalogue record for this book is available from the British Library

Printed on acid-free paper

ISBN: 978-1-78238-278-2 hardback
ISBN: 978-1-78238-279-9 institutional ebook

For Sally, Max, and Sophia

Contents

Acknowledgments ix

Introduction 1
    Three Periods of Narrative Experimentation 2
    Multiform Narratives 4
    Subjective Realism 6

Chapter 1. Complex Narratives 14
    The New Hollywood and the Smart Film 14
    New Hollywood Narration 21
    Fragmented Narratives 23
    Multi-strand Narratives 25
    Multiform Narratives 27
    Brazil 32
    Puzzle Films 34

Chapter 2. Two Trajectories of the Cinema of Attractions 39
    The Narrative Trajectory: Realism and Spectacle 41
    The Avant-Garde Trajectory: Realism and Defamiliarization 46

Chapter 3. Subjective Realism and Multiform Narratives 52
    Subjective Realism 53
    Vertigo 56
    The Fantastic 59
    Wild Strawberries 63

Chapter 4. *Mulholland Drive* 68
    Expressionism and the Uncanny in *Mulholland Drive* 69
    Three Views 74
    As Surrealist or Trance Film 75
    As Fragmented, Subjective Realist Film 78
    As Supernatural Film 84
    It Is All an Illusion 88

Chapter 5. *Memento*   94
     The Four Strands   96
     Unreliable Narration   98
     Disrupted Expectations   99
     Subjective Realism   101

Chapter 6. *Eternal Sunshine of the Spotless Mind*   112
     The Philosophy of *Eternal Sunshine*   114
     Temporal Inversions   116
     Subjective Realism   119
     Sonic Metalepsis   123
     The Marvelous Real   129

Conclusion   132

Filmography   139

Bibliography   143

Index   147

Acknowledgments

This book could not have been written without the institutional support of the University of Queensland, the Centre for Critical and Cultural Studies, and the Australian Film Television and Radio School. I would also like to specifically thank Jane Stadler, Professor Graeme Turner, Allan Cameron, and Karen Pearlman for helping make this book possible.

INTRODUCTION

In an article on narrative in contemporary cinema, *New Yorker* film critic David Denby writes about a cycle of mainstream films with complex narratives that seem more suited for the art houses than the multiplexes. Denby considers a number of these films, including *Pulp Fiction* (Quentin Tarantino 1994), *Eternal Sunshine of the Spotless Mind* (Michel Gondry 2004), and *Babel* (Alejandro González Iñárritu 2007), and situates them in relationship to their precursors in the European cinema of the fifties and sixties. He writes:

> Resnais's formalist work in the sixties was solemn and analytical. In the same period, Jean-Luc Godard, interrupting his commonplace B-movie plots with jokes, political lectures, and notes on film history, was savage and joyous. But both directors served a knowing audience, for whom experimentation was almost a norm, or at least something expected. By contrast, the recent examples of *cinéma désordonné* are meant for a mainstream audience. Suddenly life has become more interesting: when the audience's pleasure in narrative is diverted, or postponed, it may realize how conventional that pleasure usually is—how easily most movies yield to the desire for tension, release, and resolution. The kind of revelation that was once the possession of a privileged few—that formal play could not only enlarge your notion of art and entertainment but change your life—has moved out into the more volatile region of popular culture. (Denby 2007 n.p.)

Whether these kinds of narratives are providing audiences with life-changing experiences or even expanding their notions of art is debatable; what is certain, however, is that experimental narrative styles have indeed made their way into the mainstream. Films such as *Pulp Fiction* and *Inception* (Christopher Nolan 2010), for instance, have reached wider audiences than the films of Godard and Resnais ever have. In contrast to the formal experimentation of 1960s European cinema, Hollywood cinema has traditionally been characterized by its conservative style aimed at generating spectatorial absorption in narrative. Hollywood's continuity style was developed to achieve a kind of transparent immediacy through cinematography and editing techniques that promote temporal and spatial continuity in conjunction with narrative conventions that offer a clear chain of character-centered cause and effect. Filmmakers like Resnais and Godard, by contrast, employed and developed techniques that sought not to hide the mediated nature of cinema but to foreground it, often by distorting and disrupting the conventions of the continuity style in ways meant to confront or alienate spectators. Their audiences were smaller than those of Hollywood and expected to be challenged in ways that they would not be by commercial cinema. What is to be said, then, of films such as *Eternal Sunshine* and *Inception*, which are clearly aimed at mass audiences? How and why have formally complex narrative styles become fodder for mainstream films? Where does this contemporary cycle of films fit into the categories employed by critics and film scholars? And how are we to categorize films that are largely funded by studios, feature superstars like Leonardo DiCaprio, George Clooney (*Syriana* [Stephan Gaghan 2005]), Brad Pitt, and Cate Blanchett (*Babel* [Alejandro González Iñárritu 2007]), and yet significantly depart from the conventions of the traditional Hollywood style of filmmaking? These are some of the questions I want to explore in the first part of this book, and, interestingly, they are not completely new.

Three Periods of Narrative Experimentation

The use of complex narratives in Hollywood is not new; in fact, it is something of a cyclical event. A survey of the narrative trends in Hollywood cinema reveals three distinct periods of experimentation during which unconventional narrative forms have been employed in mainstream films: the first took place in the 1940s, the second in the 1960s, and the third in the 1990s. David Bordwell argues that the first period was spawned by two "trailblazing flashback movies, *Citizen Kane* [Orson Welles] and *How Green Was My Valley* [John Ford] (both 1941)" (Bordwell 2006: 73). In the years following these films, Hollywood offered a host of films with complex narratives including features such as lying flashbacks (*Crossfire*

[Edward Dmytryk 1947]), flashbacks-within-flashbacks (*The Locket* [John Brahm 1946]), subjective narration (*The Lady in the Lake* [Robert Montgomery 1947]), and unmarked ontological shifts (*Laura* [Otto Preminger 1944]) (Bordwell 2006: 72). The most commercially successful innovator of this period, Alfred Hitchcock, kills his protagonist in *Psycho* (1960), intertwines story lines connected by chance in *The Trouble with Harry* (1955), and uses flashbacks, flash-forwards, and changes in points of view in others (Bordwell 2006: 72).

In the second period of narrative experimentation, which took place from the mid 1960s to the early 1970s, directors such as Francis Ford Coppola, Martin Scorsese, and Robert Altman brought a European-inspired aesthetic into their films. The period of experimentation in the United States inspired by this is referred to as either the New Hollywood, the American New Wave, or the Hollywood Renaissance and will be considered in more detail in chapter 1. The style of "art cinema" that influenced these directors was primarily the French New Wave and the works of directors such as Bergman, Antonioni, Fellini, Kurosawa, and the like. ("Art cinema" can also be used to include "such disparate cinematic phenomena as Italian neorealism, German silent cinema, the Soviet classics, and the pre-war French cinema, from *films d'art* through surrealist works" [Cook and Bernink 1999: 106]. The term is also used to identify films that are marketed as distinct from the average Hollywood film. I will employ the term in the above ways, following scholars such as Cook and Bernink, Bordwell, and Sconce. Ultimately, however, my goal is to help refine such broad categories by offering a thorough analysis of a very particular style of narration that has emerged from the art cinema of the twentieth century.)

The third period of narrative experimentation arguably began in the mid 1990s after the unexpected success of "independent" films such as *Pulp Fiction* and *The English Patient* (Anthony Minghella 1996), the narrative styles of which were unusually complex for the mainstream audiences who made them successful—demonstrating that not only were tastes changing, but that, as in other areas of popular culture, the formerly clear boundaries between the aesthetics of high art and those of commercial forms were not as clear as they once were. In the United States, this blurring of boundaries bled over into the industry as well, as many independent film production and/or distribution companies such as Miramax were acquired by multinational media corporations seeking to capitalize on this thriving sector of the industry, particularly after the box-office success of *Pulp Fiction*. It is this third period of narrative experimentation that is the primary focus of this book, which will specifically address the question of how to conceptualize and categorize the complex narrative styles of a diverse group of films including but not limited to films such as *Memento* (Christopher Nolan 2000), *Mulholland Drive* (David Lynch 2001), *Eternal Sunshine*, *The Fountain* (Darren Aronofsky 2006), *Stranger than Fiction* (Marc Forster 2006), *Inception*, and *Source Code* (Duncan Jones 2011) (as well as many other related films in the cycle).

A range of reasons has been offered for the emergence of these films. David Bordwell, for instance, cites the boom in independent production of the 1980s and 1990s, arguing that narrative complexity became a way of marketing certain movies as distinct from run-of-the-mill Hollywood fare (2006: 74). This explanation provides some idea of why filmmakers and distributors invested time and money in these films, but it does not explain why audiences paid to see them. For this, Bordwell turns to other factors, including the fact that younger audiences raised on cable television and video games craved the novelty offered by films with complex narratives such as *The Matrix* (Andy Wachowski and Lana Wachowski 1999) (Bordwell 2006: 74). Other reasons complex narrative forms have migrated from the art houses of Europe and New York City to the multiplexes of Memphis and Taipei is that access to alternative cinema has increased as a result of new technologies. Digital technology has made accessing films from outside Hollywood much easier than in the past, giving audiences much wider exposure to unconventional forms of cinema, which may also contribute to a willingness to endure the challenges presented by films with unconventional narratives. These technologies have had an influence in other ways as well, and scholars like Alison McMahan and Marsha Kinder have argued that the influence of databases, video games, multiuser domains, and online gaming have contributed to the changing narrative styles of mainstream cinema. While this influence seems obvious, assertions by scholars such as Kinder that link the popularity of complex narrative films to the influence of video games or cyber-narrative often overstate this influence (2006: 74). By contrast, I will argue that the cycle of complex narrative cinema that began in the 1990s has been influenced less by databases or cyber-fiction than by the complex narratives of the cinema of the twentieth century.

Multiform Narratives

Now, returning to the problem of classification raised by these films. To call *Eternal Sunshine* a comedy or *Babel* a melodrama is not incorrect. However, neither of these categories offers a very rich description of these films. Critics such as Denby have refrained from creating labels for either the specific styles of the films or the more general cycle of which they are a part, whereas film scholars have proven far less reluctant. Bordwell, for instance, in a series of articles and books on films with complex narratives, has employed a new set of terms for these films that includes *forking-path* and *multiple-draft narratives, subjective stories, network stories,* and *multiple-protagonist* and *converging-fate films*. Warren Buckland's *Puzzle Films: Complex Storytelling in Contemporary Cinema* (2009), a collection of wide-ranging articles on films with complex narratives, also employs a set of terms including *puzzle films, mind-game films,* and *twist films*. Each of these emphasizes different aspects of the complex films it describes and is useful and illuminating in the contexts in which it is used. There are, however, still gaps in the conceptual work as well as a lack of specificity in some of the analysis, which has led to a profusion of labels and categories. The lack of specificity frustrates attempts to catalogue the narrative styles of the recent wave of complex films, and a simple example of this can be seen in the critical work on *Memento,* a favorite of scholars working on complex narrative films. *Memento* has been called a "twist film" (Wilson 2006), a "puzzle film" (Buckland 2009), a "mind-game film" (Elsaesser 2009), and a "subjective story" (Bordwell 2003). Each of these scholars offers unique insights into particular facets of the film and their categories are undeniably useful. The problem, however, is that with each new analysis comes a new label for the film. To date, there are no agreed-upon narratological categories in which to place films such as *Memento*. Most importantly, the terms that are used to describe *Memento*'s narrative structure are often rather general, so, although it been given multiple labels based on its different attributes (nonlinear temporality, unreliable narration), it is invariably situated in a category among a host of other films with which it has very little in common. In light of these problems, it seems that a more specific narrative taxonomy needs to be developed and employed to account for the unconventional narrative forms that are emerging in the cinema. This can be done by modifying and refining current narrative taxonomies and employing terms and categories useful in a wide range of contexts.

The goal of this book is to offer such modifications. The refinements it proposes have grown, in part, out of an analysis of a range of films with complex narratives including *Mulholland Drive, Memento,* and *Eternal Sunshine of the Spotless Mind*. These films were chosen on the basis of a narrative structure they share with antecedents from German Expressionist and surrealist cinema, from films from various movements of the 1950s and 60s, as well as from a number of films from Hollywood. Many of these precursors will be considered here, along with more contemporary examples of films that employ the structure in question, which I will call *multiform narrative*. The concept of the multiform narrative comes from the work of Janet Murray and has proven immensely useful for me in refining the broad categories of complex narratives in two key ways. First, the term designates a specific type of narrative on the basis of a structural feature: multiple ontologies. This is useful because it delineates the multiform narrative from the *unified narrative structure*, the default mode of storytelling in commercial cinema for over a century, and the *multi-strand narrative structure*, a more complex narrative form that often features multiple protagonists. Multiform narratives are different from unified narratives in that they employ multiple narrative strands, yet they also differ from multi-strand narratives in their use of mixed or multiple ontologies. The second and related reason that Murray's term is useful is that it can be used to categorize not only recent examples of multiform films, but also a number of international art cinema films that precede them, including *The Cabinet of Dr. Caligari* (Robert Weine 1919), *Un Chien Andalou* (Buñuel 1927), *Rashomon* (Akira Kurosawa 1951), *Wild Strawberries* (Ingmar Bergman 1957), and *8½* (Federico Fellini 1962). This second aspect of the category of the multiform is important, because it provides a flexibility not provided by categories such as "art cinema" or "modernist cinema," which do not fit many recent multiform films that come out of very different cultural, industrial, and historical contexts. Yet, as we shall see, these contemporary multiform films do share many narrative and aesthetic characteristics with earlier films that have become exemplars of "modernist cinema" and/or "art cinema." Categorizing such films under the rubric "multiform cinema," then, enables a comparison of films across movements and time periods on the basis of a shared structural feature, multiple ontologies.

Subjective Realism

Multiform cinema as a category, however, has limitations of its own, the most important of which is that it includes a very large number of films that fall outside the parameters of complex narrative cinema. As such, it is too large a category to be dealt with comprehensively in these pages. In order to limit the focus and scope of this work and avoid the risk of merely adding to the already overcrowded field of general analysis of complex narrative, what this book will do is focus on a decidedly small group of films that share multiform narratives of a very specific type. This choice has led to the creation of a specific subcategory of the multiform based on the identification of a trait that unifies the films I am interested in working with (as well as linking them to a tradition of films from the art cinema to which they are indebted). The trait is what will be called *subjective realism* and refers to the fact that at least one of the film's dual or multiple strands represents the subjective perspective of its central character (Bordwell 1985: 206). Subjective realism is a term borrowed from David Bordwell but has direct parallels to what Bruce F. Kawin (1978) refers to as the "mindscreen" and what Edward Branigan calls "deep internal focalization" (1992: 87).

To understand the way in which I will use this term, consider *Mulholland Drive*, which has two narrative strands. Both offer the first-person perspective of its central character, Diane Selwyn, whose deteriorating psyche is the source of the film's unreliable narration; consequently, *Mulholland Drive* offers its viewer no objective level of narration in the film. *Memento* also features subjective realist narrative strands that are motivated by an attempt to place the spectator in an epistemological position similar to the one created by the anterograde amnesia of its central character, Leonard Shelby (Guy Pearce). And *Eternal Sunshine of the Spotless Mind*'s humorous disruptions of time, space, and narrative logic are meant to represent the experience of its central character, Joel Barish, as his memory is being systematically annihilated. The subjective realist style of narration used in each of these films has long been employed in the international art cinema in a similar manner, and what follows in these pages is an argument for the recognition of this tradition of filmmaking *as a tradition,* which dates back to at least 1919. The body of work represented will be referred to as the *subjective realist multiform cinema.*

Chapter 1 will begin by situating the contemporary multiform films central to this cycle in the industrial and institutional contexts of the New Hollywood. To do this, it will consider the relationships among Hollywood, art cinema, and American independent cinema in order to better understand the contemporary context from which the current cycle of American complex narrative films has emerged. Many of these films, although "independent" in some way, were partially financed and/or distributed by a major studio or subsidiary. Add to this the fact that many of them employ conventions more common to European art cinema than to mainstream Hollywood and yet have reached mainstream audiences, and we are back to the question of classification considered above: *What kinds of films are these?* In my answer to this question I argue that these contemporary multiform films are best understood as examples of what Jeffrey Sconce calls "smart films," a class of American "independent" film related to international art cinema, but still closely tied to the major studios. After this brief exploration of these industrial aspects of American independent cinema, chapter 1 will consider the narrative forms commonly employed in independent cinema. In the process, it will argue that there is a gap in the current narrative taxonomies and demonstrate that, although much recent work has focused on complex narrative in the cinema, there is still much more to be done. More specifically, it will argue that even though many scholars have analyzed the three keys films I am examining, the extremely useful concept of the "multiform" has been overlooked. This is partially understandable given that the pioneering work of Janet Murray and Alison McMahan on the subject has situated multiform narrative primarily in its relation to cyber-narrative and game theory. While these avenues may be important to the study of contemporary cinema, they have not necessarily proven crucial or relevant for scholars seeking to understand the cycle of films with complex narratives. Yet, multiform narrative as defined by Murray is a useful concept, and chapter 1 will argue that the gap in current narrative taxonomies (both those of independent cinema and "complex narrative" cinema more generally) can be partially mended using Murray's category. Chapter 1 will draw on Murray's definition and demonstrate its applicability, arguing that as a narrative category, the multiform provides a way of making useful distinctions within existing narratological frameworks. These distinctions allow for the identification and articulation of the fine differences that set multiform narrative apart from similar styles of narrative.

Chapters 2 and 3 will explore the aesthetic and narrative conventions of narrative cinema in order to better understand the way in which multiform cinema relates to the continuity style of classical Hollywood and the way in which it challenges this style using various forms of defamiliarization. In these chapters, it will be argued that the notion of a subjective realist multiform cinema can be applied retrospectively to a small body of films from the art cinema of the twentieth century, including but not limited to *Caligari*, *Wild Strawberries*, and *8½*. Further, it will be shown that the roots of this multiform cinema can be understood in terms of their relationship to what Tom Gunning has referred to as the "cinema of attractions" (1990), particularly the way in which the trick photography and other techniques developed by George Méliès were later put to use by avant-garde filmmakers. Chapter 2 will argue that the subjective realist multiform cinema employs similar techniques in ways that disrupt immersion and draw attention to the transparent window that the continuity style seeks to create. The exhibitionistic style will be contrasted with the voyeuristic style employed in narrative cinema, and although the exhibitionism/voyeurism binary will ultimately be problematized, the contrast between these two styles of filmmaking will serve as a framework for a brief exploration of Gunning's two trajectories of the cinema of attractions—the avant-garde and the mainstream—and I will argue that the subjective realist multiform cinema has roots in the avant-garde trajectory of the cinema of attractions.

As a contemporary form of the cinema of attractions, multiform films will be shown to have affinities with the blockbuster in that they use complex narratives to create a type of cinematic pyrotechnics that seeks to compete with the spectacle employed in the blockbuster, yet it is ultimately the differences between the two that are of interest. The subjective realist multiform film is distinct from these mainstream Hollywood films in several ways. First, they are distinct in terms of their budgets, their casts, and the marketing strategies used to sell them. So, unlike the blockbuster, multiform smart films have small production and promotion budgets and generally do not feature expensive forms of spectacle or stars (*Eternal Sunshine* being an exception). Second, subjective realist multiform films are distinct from Hollywood multiform blockbusters such as *The Matrix* in their use of naturalistic settings: the alternate realities of the subjective realist multiform films are not futuristic or otherworldly, but "real" worlds of the more here and now, albeit set in the interior spaces of their central character's mind. Although there have been examples of such subjective realist narration in mainstream films such as *A Beautiful Mind* (Ron Howard 2001), they are rare. Ultimately, it will be argued that these contemporary instances of the subjective realist multiform film can be situated in a class of film that I will call the low-budget cinema of attractions. Further, it is on the basis of the success of these films that Hollywood studios have backed larger-budget films such as *The Fountain* and *Inception*, which will be considered below as representing the culmination of the current cycle.

Chapter 3 will focus on a particular narrative technique used in subjective realist multiform cinema: subjective realist narration. The subjective realist style of narration has been employed in multiform films from *Caligari* to *Inception* and was developed as an alternative to the classical Hollywood style. It has often been used in ways deliberately meant to blur ontological boundaries, disrupting the voyeuristic transparency of the classical style. Disruptions of time, space, and causality are not out of place in dreams, memories, and hallucinations—and consequently, the laws that govern realist styles of narration do not apply in subjective realist narration. Its effectiveness results from the fact that, as a style, it is used to represent what is taking place in the mind of a character, where the laws of the natural world do not necessarily apply.

Chapters 4 through 6 will offer analysis of three subjective realist multiform films: *Mulholland Drive*, *Memento*, and *Eternal Sunshine*. These films were chosen for several reasons: each employs a multiform narrative in which at least one strand represents the subjective realist perspective of its central character; each represents a different point on the continuum of narrative complexity (with *Mulholland Drive* at one end of the continuum, *Memento* at the center, and *Eternal Sunshine* at the other end); and finally, each can be seen as an example of the low-budget cinema of attractions.

Chapter 4 will consider *Mulholland Drive*, which is one of the few films that have been theorized specifically as instances of multiform film. *Mulholland Drive* provides a clear example of the way in which multiform narratives are used to create complexity by combining a multi-strand narrative with alternate ontologies and with spatial, temporal, and ontological fragmentation. Additionally, because of its narrative ambiguity, *Mulholland Drive* has been seen by some critics as sitting on the border between experimental and narrative cinema; so, in this sense, *Mulholland Drive* serves as a limit case of the multiform feature film, closer on the continuum to the films of Resnais or Antonioni than to those of Hollywood. Finally, *Mulholland Drive* has attracted a wide variety of attention from scholars of numerous theoretical backgrounds and, therefore, provides a good introduction to some of the many ways of approaching multiform cinema and the issues it raises.

Mulholland Drive will be analyzed in terms of its two major narrative strands, which are presented separately in what I will call two movements. It will be argued that these movements represent the film's two major ontological frames of reference: the oneiric and the psychotic. The first movement represents a dream of the film's central character, Diane Selwyn (Naomi Watts), who is refigured in the dream as "Betty Elms," a naïve young Canadian who arrives in Hollywood to pursue a career as an actress. Betty befriends the mysterious amnesiac "Rita," who has survived a murder attempt but lost her memory in the ensuing violence. This first movement contains several other minor narrative strands as well, including The Man Who Dies of Fright, A Day in the Life of Adam Dresher, and The Story of the Bumbling Hit-Man (Andrews 2004: 25). These micronarratives make the first movement of *Mulholland Drive* a multi-strand narrative in and of itself. *Mulholland Drive*'s second movement begins after the enigmatic conclusion of movement one and represents the last hours of the guilt-ridden and psychotic Diane Selwyn, who awakens from her dream only to be overwhelmed by the guilt she is experiencing over her part in the murder of her former lover. One of the many difficulties faced by viewers of *Mulholland Drive* arises from the fragmentation of this second movement, which features radical disruptions of time, space, and causality, as well as including seemingly unexplainable occurrences. Another results from the fact that the narrative boundaries between *Mulholland Drive*'s ontologically distinct spheres cannot be identified—unlike those of *Eternal Sunshine* or *Memento*, which are finally identifiable—and, therefore, the film presents a much more difficult challenge to those who would make meaning from its fragmented plot. However, it will be argued that the fragmentation and marvelous elements of the film follow from the fact that it represents Diane's oneiric and psychotic mental states from her own perspective and that when this subjective realist approach is taken, a strong case can be made for a coherent reading of the film.

Chapter 5 will focus on Christopher Nolan's *Memento*, a multiform thriller that can be seen as pioneering a style of narration I will refer to as *progressive analepsis*. Although the innovative temporal space created for the film is relevant to the exploration of *Memento*'s subjective realist narration, it is not what makes the film an example of multiform cinema. What does are the subjective realist alternate realities that make up several of *Memento*'s "flashback" sequences, two of which will be analyzed and shown to be fictional. I will argue that *Memento*'s lying flashbacks are used to mislead spectators and to subvert narrative expectations in a shocking manner. Although *Memento*'s narration is innovative, I will argue that the twist is derived from techniques developed in the subjective realist multiform strand of the art cinema. Like that of *Mulholland Drive*'s Diane Selwyn, *Memento*'s Leonard Shelby's experience of the world is atypical, and the goal of the narration is to render this experience in a manner that allows spectators to vicariously experience it as well.

Memento will also be considered in terms of its four distinct narrative strands. The first presents, in reverse order, the main events surrounding the murder of James "Teddy" Gammel (Joe Pantoliano). Teddy is murdered by Leonard Shelby, the central character of the film, who suffers from a condition called anterograde amnesia. His condition, which makes it impossible for him to form new memories, was brought on by a head injury suffered during a robbery of his home (spectators are also led to believe that Leonard's wife was raped and killed during this robbery). The retrogressive analeptic structure of this central narrative strand is intended to re-create for spectators the disorientation that Leonard himself experiences as a result of his condition. The inversion of cause and effect created by the narration is central to the powerful subversion of expectations that takes place late in the film. *Memento*'s second strand is a black-and-white sequence representing a phone conversation between Leonard and (presumably) Teddy, which takes place at the beginning of the story but is presented intermittently throughout the film. The conversation is used as voice-over narration in some cases and resembles the type of narration often employed in *film noir*. The third strand is a flashback that represents Leonard's unreliable account of The Story of Sammy Jankis, another sufferer of anterograde amnesia whose case Leonard oversaw for the insurance company he worked for before his accident. Leonard recounts this story during the phone conversation in the second strand, so the story is presented as an embedded narrative, framed by the conversation. In a related fourth strand, Leonard's (again unreliable) account of his relationship with his wife is presented in fragments throughout the main strand.

The combination of lying flashbacks and a retrogressive analeptic temporality makes *Memento* a unique example of the multiform film. Its many unconventional techniques create an uncanny film-viewing experience for spectators and situate it firmly in the contemporary low-budget cinema of attractions. Unlike *Mulholland Drive*, however, *Memento* has found audiences outside of the art houses of Europe and America, and I will argue that this is largely a result of the fact that, like *Eternal Sunshine*, *Memento* is a complex, but mostly comprehensible, narrative film.

Chapter 6 will consider *Eternal Sunshine of the Spotless Mind*, arguably the most accessible, and without a doubt the most commercially successful, of the three contemporary examples of the subjective realist multiform film. *Eternal Sunshine* had the largest production budget of the three films and features Hollywood stars Jim Carrey and Kate Winslet. Regardless, *Eternal Sunshine* remains an example of the low-budget smart cinema of attractions. It uses a subjective realist multiform narrative to create a complex and unconventional experience for spectators. It features two major narrative strands: one that I will call the waking strand, and the other, the subjective realist strand. The first tells the story of Joel Barish (Jim Carrey), whose girlfriend, Clementine Kruczynski (Kate Winslet), has had all memory of him erased by a new technology developed by an organization called the Lacuna Company. When Joel learns what Clementine has done, he is devastated and decides to undertake the procedure himself. In this waking strand of *Eternal Sunshine*, the narrative structure is reasonably stable: cause and effect follow the patterns of classical narration, a realistic space is established and maintained through continuity editing techniques, and temporally—though the film is not linear—it has what might be called a false linearity: false because the major temporal gaps of the early part of the film are not evident until later. However, in the subjective realist strand that follows—which represents the erasure of Joel's memory from inside his mind and is ontologically distinct from the waking world—the rules of classical narration are bracketed, resulting in major disruptions of causality, time, and space. This produces disruptions much like those found in *Mulholland Drive*, *Memento*, and numerous other subjective realist multiform films. I will argue, however, that unlike both *Mulholland Drive* and *Memento, Eternal Sunshine* is wholly recoupable in narrative terms. It resolves all of the enigmas it raises and offers the type of closure audiences have come to expect from Hollywood cinema. As such, it is the most conservative of the three case studies and, not surprisingly, has been the most commercially successful of the three.

Chapter 1

COMPLEX NARRATIVES

The goal of this chapter is to situate the films that are the focus of my analysis in the institutional, economic, and narrative contexts of contemporary Hollywood. This will be done in two stages. The first will explore the changes in the American filmmaking industry that have produced the New Hollywood. The second stage will focus on the narrative forms common to the contemporary American "independent" sector of this New Hollywood, offering an explanation of fragmented and multi-strand narratives. In doing so, I will offer a definition of the multiform narrative, the structure used in films from *The Cabinet of Dr. Caligari* to *Eternal Sunshine of the Spotless Mind*. The multiform narratives of these films are used in conjunction with a subjective realist mode of narration to create what I am calling *subjective realist multiform narrative*.

The New Hollywood and the Smart Film

There are two common uses of the term "New Hollywood." Initially, it was used to refer to the art cinema–influenced period of aesthetic and narrative experimentation of the 1960s and early 1970s; however, it is also commonly used to denote the shifts in Hollywood filmmaking and distribution practices in the post–World War II era. In describing the latter, Thomas Schatz distinguishes the structures of production and distribution of films in postwar America from those that preceded them by contrasting the contemporary system with the studio or classical

Hollywood system of the twenties, thirties, and forties (1993: 8). This transition from the studio system to the "New Hollywood" was largely the result of two key factors: the advent of television and the dismantling of the studios' monopoly on production, distribution, and exhibition—a practice referred to as vertical integration. The "New Hollywood," in this sense, refers to both a new era of filmmaking as well as new economic and institutional structures. Thomas Elsaesser makes similar use of the term when he writes: "Three elements make up the 'New Hollywood,' first, a new generation of directors (sometimes called 'Movie Brats'), second, new marketing strategies (centered on the blockbuster as a distribution and exhibition concept), and third, new media ownership and management styles in the film industry" (1998: 191). Elsaesser's inclusion of both blockbusters and new directors in his description alludes to the changes in style often associated with the transition. The New Hollywood will be used here to refer to *both* aesthetic and industrial shifts in American cinema in the years since the Paramount Decree (the Supreme Court ruling that ended vertical integration); it is, then, a periodizing term that encompasses various changes, as well as continuities, in postwar American cinema.

The multiform films that are the primary focus of this book have emerged since the late 1990s, primarily from the independent sector of this New Hollywood. Like their American New Wave predecessors from the 1960s, these films are different from more mainstream Hollywood productions in two ways: first, they were produced on significantly smaller budgets, and second, they use aesthetic and narrative conventions common to European art cinema. This study will consider the narrative challenges and pleasures offered by this cycle of independent multiform films as well as demonstrate the power of mainstream cinema to incorporate and domesticate innovative and challenging forms into its ever-expanding narrative and generic stable. Hollywood's willingness to vary its forms is not new, of course, as we have already seen in the introduction, which identified three significant periods of narrative experimentation, including the present one, launched in the 1990s. It is this period of experimentation (roughly 1994–2012) that will be the primary focus of this investigation; however, the roots of this cycle of films in the art cinema of the past century will be explored as well. The contemporary American independent cinema context from which these instances of multiform films have emerged is significant both industrially and aesthetically since it serves to set the films apart from their more mainstream rivals. As such, they represent an important facet of what has come to be known as the New Hollywood. My choice to focus on the American independent cinema for examples is a result of the fact that it is from this context that many of the groundbreaking films of the cycle have emerged.[1] Without *Pulp Fiction*, for instance, it seems very unlikely that this spate of complex narrative films from around the globe would exist, much less be reaching the wide audiences they are.

In this sense, this period of narrative experimentation is not unlike earlier periods, when the commercial success of one or two films sparked a chain reaction of narrative experimentation. For example, in the years between the dismantling of studios' oligopoly on the film industry and rise of the blockbuster (roughly 1948–1975), access to films from outside the Hollywood system grew. As the studios' hold on distribution and exhibition loosened, art-house cinemas and university film societies flourished across the United States, introducing audiences to foreign films as well as opening new markets for American independent films. In 1960, Federico Fellini's *La Dolce Vita* and Alfred Hitchcock's *Psycho* were surprise box-office hits, and the commercial success of these films was a contributing factor in the opening up of a window of opportunity for a group of young American filmmakers—including Robert Altman, Mike Nichols, Francis Ford Coppola, and Martin Scorsese—to experiment with a European art cinema–influenced aesthetic. In addition to this, "A growing contingent of international auteurs—Bergman, Fellini, Truffaut, Bertolucci, Polanski, Kubrick—who, in the wake of the 1966 success of Antonioni's *Blow Up* and Claude Lelouch's *A Man and a Woman*, developed a quasi-independent relationship with Hollywood, making films for a Euro-American market and bringing the art cinema into the mainstream" (Schatz 1993: 14). The youth market was, in part, responsible for these trends, as were the social and political upheavals of the late 1960s. The success of films like *The Graduate* (Mike Nichols 1968), *2001: A Space Odyssey* (Stanley Kubrick 1968), and *Easy Rider* (Dennis Hopper 1969) provides evidence of shifting audiences and tastes, as well as reflecting the potential for niche marketing after the replacement of the Production Code with a ratings system. Unfortunately, many of these changes were not to last. This is because at the same time as the shift in cinematic taste was taking place, more Americans were moving to the suburbs and turning to their television sets for entertainment. Movie attendance dropped to new lows, and despite the individual successes of these more experimental films, many studios were verging on bankruptcy: "Feature filmmaking continued to hemorrhage money—by some estimates, as much as half a billion dollars between 1969 and 1972" (Bordwell 2006: 2).

In the mid 1970s, however, the tremendous commercial success of a very different type of film revived the major studios and provided the impetus for a revolution in production and marketing strategies that would reshape the New Hollywood (as well as bring an end to the aesthetic and narrative experimentation of the "American New Wave"). Although it was *The Godfather* (1972) that rescued Paramount from bankruptcy, it was the phenomenal box-office success of *Jaws* in 1975 (Spielberg) and *Star Wars* in 1977 (Lucas) that signaled the arrival of the blockbuster and the industrial changes that would follow in its wake.

> While one crucial dimension of the New Hollywood is the "space" that has been opened for independent and alternative cinema, the fact is that these mainstream hits [blockbusters] are where stars, genres and cinematic innovations invariably are established, where the "grammar" of cinema is most likely to be refined, and where the essential qualities of the medium—its popular and commercial character—are most evident. These blockbuster hits are, for better or worse, what the New Hollywood is about, and thus are the necessary starting point for any analysis of contemporary American cinema. (Schatz 1993: 10–11)

While the blockbuster has indeed become the mainstay of the New Hollywood, it will be argued here that is *not* the space where the "grammar" of cinema is refined (particularly not the narrative grammar). The blockbuster's rise followed from the phenomenal revenues generated by *Jaws* and *Star Wars* and led studios to shift their business strategies toward an allocation of vast resources for the production and promotion of the must-see event film. The formula evolved through the 1980s and 1990s into the high-risk tent-pole strategy in which the success or failure of an immensely expensive blockbuster can often determine the fates of numerous smaller budget productions, and this remains a central characteristic of the industry at present.

Blockbusters are often based on a presold property such as a popular novel, comic book, or video game. They are released at Christmas or during summer holidays and shown on thousands of screens worldwide. Their promotion budgets often match or even exceed their production budgets, and the merchandising of products related to the film can sometimes generate revenues that rival or even exceed those of the box office. Aesthetically, blockbusters are, more often than not, centered on attractions such as spectacular special effects sequences. Schatz, like many other critics, has lamented the rise of this style of filmmaking, viewing it as a commercial enterprise with little artistic merit, featuring "one-dimensional characters, mechanical plots, [and] high-gloss style," in short, spectacle over substance (1993: 33). This is a common criticism of the blockbuster, and in its most reduced form, is based on the spectacle/narrative binary that has been at the center of numerous important debates in screen studies over the previous decades. This binary is relevant here since I will argue that subjective realist multiform films were born as a kind of low-budget cinema of attractions, featuring what can be understood to be the narrative answer to spectacle. Many of the multiform films considered use complex narratives to create novel, unpredictable, and at times, shocking events and twists that offer spectators pleasures meant to compete with those offered by blockbusters.

Although the rise of the blockbuster signaled the end of an era of mainstream narrative experimentation, it was also the beginning of a new era of independent film production, which was initially defined by yet another new generation of independent filmmakers who honed their skills in the truly low-budget shadow of the blockbuster. Filmmakers such as Jim Jarmusch, Spike Lee, and Hal Hartley are among the directors of this period whose independent films kept the independent sector alive. In his seminal article on the New Hollywood, Schatz writes, "We might see the New Hollywood as producing three different classes of movie: the calculated blockbuster designed with the multimedia marketplace and franchise status in mind; the mainstream A-class star-vehicle with sleeper-hit potential, and the low-cost independent feature targeted for a specific market and with little chance of anything more than 'cult film' status" (1993: 35). Although there have been some significant changes in the industry since Schatz wrote, this threefold division remains quite useful when considering contemporary American cinema. From the late 1970s on, blockbusters have indeed tied up larger and larger portions of studio production budgets; regardless of this, American independent filmmaking thrived both economically and aesthetically at different times during this period. This was the result of several factors, including the fall in the number of films produced by the majors, new markets opened for films by cable television, and the growing demand for video and then DVD rentals. Another important factor was the aggressive marketing strategies employed by independent film distributors like Miramax, which resulted in several independent films generating blockbuster-like revenues during the 1990s and shattering the notion that the most that could be expected from an independent film was "cult status." *Pulp Fiction*, for example, grossed over U.S. $100 million on its theatrical release alone, and shortly thereafter, Miramax's *The English Patient* clearly demonstrated that *Pulp Fiction* was not an isolated case. The result was not unlike the one that followed the success of *Jaws*, and a rapid transformation of the structure of the American film industry took place. In addition, the complex narratives of these two Miramax films paved the way for a flood of others with similarly complex narratives.[2]

The most important result of the transformation was the takeover of independent distributors by large media conglomerates in the 1990s. Miramax, for example, was purchased by Disney, New Line by Time

Warner, and October Films (ultimately) by Universal. The result of these takeovers was a significant reduction in the autonomy of what once was the independent filmmaking sector of the industry. Presently, few if any independently produced feature films are released without some involvement of the major studios, particularly at the level of distribution. The label "Independent American Cinema" has thus become a marketing tool—a way of offering audiences an alternative to the blockbuster or star vehicle—and now functions more to differentiate products than to signal creative independence. In other words, it can be viewed as something of a nonsensical designation. A further consequence of these changes has been that the production costs of "independent" features have risen considerably. Distributors and production companies, in an effort to raise presales of independent films, have begun to cast stars and hire marketable directors. Screenplays based on popular novels or written by star screenwriters like Charlie Kaufman further increase costs. The goal, of course, is to re-create the blockbuster-like box-office returns of earlier films such as *Pulp Fiction* or *The English Patient*. The downside of this push for the "quality indie blockbuster," however, is that higher budgets, although still much lower than the industry average, have resulted in fewer being made.[3]

The upside is that on the aesthetic level, the "independent" feature film continues to be a site of experimentation where new forms are developed and refined. This is because even though independent films have increasingly had to operate under the commercial imperatives of the studios, they remain distinct from both blockbusters and star vehicles, and have, to some extent, maintained a unique aesthetic role in the industry. As the Hollywood auteurs helped shape the cinema of the 1960s and 1970s, so have the independent directors of the 1980s and 1990s helped shape the cinema of the early part of the new century. Subjective realist multiform films such as *Memento* and *Eternal Sunshine,* for instance, were both produced by independent production companies on budgets well below that of the industry average; yet, both performed extremely well at the box office, recouping their costs several times over.[4] In addition, both have cult followings and significant DVD sales (a crucial aspect of the economic forces driving the New Hollywood). Aesthetically, both of these films feature complex narrative forms that demand much more from audiences than their mainstream counterparts, and *Mulholland Drive,* which began as a pilot for a television show, was transformed, after being purchased by European interests, into a highly complex feature film.[5] As David Denby has argued in "The New Disorder" (2007: n.p.), the pleasures these complex films offer have much more in common with those offered by art cinema than classical Hollywood. Their moderate commercial success, like the success of films such as *sex, lies, and videotape* (Steven Soderbergh 1989), demonstrates that there are indeed audiences for more challenging films and ensures that more like them will certainly follow. Critics and scholars, however, disagree over how to categorize them and others like them. Are they really independent films? Studio films? Art films? What?

Scholar Jeffrey Sconce offers a useful way of thinking through some of the difficulties raised by the new industrial arrangements of the contemporary American independent cinema and identifies a trend within the New Hollywood that he calls "smart cinema," which he characterizes as follows: "Taken together, these admittedly disparate yet often ideologically sympathetic films suggest an interesting shift in the strategies of contemporary 'art cinema,' here defined as movies marketed in explicit counter-distinction to mainstream Hollywood fare as 'smarter' 'artier,' and more 'independent' (however questionable and manufactured such distinctions might actually be)" (Sconce 2002: 350). Although the most common feature of the "smart films" he discusses is their shared target market of young, educated, bohemian audiences, there are aesthetic, stylistic, and tonal similarities as well (Sconce 2002: 351). Smart films, according to Sconce, have replaced the social politics of the art films of the 1960s and 1970s with "the 'personal politics' of power, communication, emotional dysfunction and identity in white middle-class culture" (351); and although Sconce compares the general narrative tendencies of the smart film to those of the international art cinema, he also argues this: "While previous forms of art cinema concentrated on formal experimentation with film style and narrative structure as a means of critiquing codes of 'bourgeois realism' and/or 'bourgeois society,' the new smart cinema has for the most part re-embraced classical narrative strategies, instead experimenting with tone as a means of critiquing bourgeois taste and culture" (Sconce 2002: 351–52).

While this re-embracing of classical narrative may be true of many or most of the films he discusses, there are also a large number of films coming from the same industrial location, marketed to the same educated, bespectacled, bohemian audiences that do indeed experiment with narrative. These films have pushed the boundaries of cinematic realism, much like the films of the Hollywood auteurs of the 1960s and 1970s did. Sconce himself lists several of these in his catalogue of "smart films," including *Slacker* (Richard Linklater 1991), *Magnolia* (P.T. Anderson 1998), *Being John Malkovich* (Spike Jonze 1999), and *Donnie Darko* (Richard Kelly 2001). It is these types of independent films that have led Bordwell to identify the 1990s as an important period of narrative experimentation.[6] The smart film label is, then, in Sconce's own use, inclusive of films with unconventional narratives, and many, if not all, of the multiform films I will explore in this book can be seen as having a close relationship to his "smart film."

What I would like to do now is analyze, in very broad strokes, some of the styles of complex narration common in the American independent cinema and, ultimately, in the multiform smart films that are the focus of this book. I have two goals in what remains of this chapter: the first is to demonstrate that there is a gap in the taxonomy[7] of narrative forms used in independent cinema (and increasingly, in cinema more widely), and the second is to propose a category that will partially mend this gap.[8]

New Hollywood Narration

As Sconce writes of smart cinema, the primary mode of narration in independent cinema *is* the Hollywood style. When independent films do depart from the classical style, however, the departures often resemble those common in the international art cinema.[9] For instance, surrealist and Expressionist filmmakers, as well as directors from the various new wave movements of the 1960s and 1970s, developed their own narrative and aesthetic conventions, often in direct opposition to the classical narrative style. David Bordwell, in his exploration of art-cinema narration, notes that filmmakers within this tradition have often critiqued previous cinematic conventions and justified novelty as "a new realism" (Bordwell 1985: 206). Robert Stam examines numerous such responses to Hollywood in his *Film and Theory*, including the French New Wave (which attacked the artificiality of Hollywood "realism"), and the Italian neorealist movement (which sought to show the true face of postwar Italy via its documentary-style social realism) (Stam 2000b: 224). These are simply two of the many examples of the way in which the art cinema of twentieth century challenged the status quo of mainstream cinema. The realism that is often the target of these challenges is rooted in the literary realism of the nineteenth century, and privileges narrative coherence and stable individual identities. As a style, its realism is generated by three key characteristics: a clear chain of causality, a high degree of resolution, and continuity editing. In classical Hollywood narration, characters function as causes. These characters are clearly motivated to solve a well-defined problem and to act according to psychological traits that are evident and generally consistent. The canonical film generally begins with a state of equilibrium that is then disrupted. This disruption is what motivates the central character's quest, and the story ends shortly after the restoration of equilibrium. In the classical cinema, editing is primarily concerned with realism and follows the conventions that produce the most unobtrusive use of shot transitions (Elsaesser and Buckland 2002: 36–37). The continuity style seeks to hide edits and maintain a smooth, unbroken temporal and spatial continuity across a film—focusing attention on story and characters. Key features of this style are the 180 degree system and analytic editing, both of which feature the use of establishing shots, shot/reverse shots (for dialogue), eyeline matches, and matches on action. This Hollywood style of realism is the background against which art cinema conventions and innovations should be considered. This is because this style is, for the most part, the default style of commercial filmmaking the world over. The innovations of art cinema are often offered as more authentic representations of the world than the realism of the Hollywood style. (In chapters 2 and 3, I will present a more detailed analysis of art-cinema aesthetics and narration than I offer here, where my goal has been to describe the narrative milieu from which the contemporary multiform films I am considering emerge.)

Geoff King, in seeking to align American independent cinema with the art-cinema tradition, writes that independent films question "the objective cause/effect definition of reality and identity offered by the classical style" and present "a realism based on a different conception of the nature of reality, one that is more contingent and in which events are more open-ended and tenuously linked" (2005: 101–2). King explores the narrative conventions employed by these films through a Bordwellian framework, and as I will also draw from Bordwell's framework for my analysis of the subjective realist multiform film, a brief explanation of it is in order here. Key to Bordwell's theory is its consideration of both the way in which a film is structured and the way in which it is perceived. It focuses not simply on the elements that make up a film, but also on the way in which the audience makes sense of these elements. His theory of narrative borrows from cognitive psychology, "which studies how perceivers 'make sense' of the world from inherently fragmentary and incomplete data and experience. For example, we can only directly see three sides of a six-sided solid cube. But from this incomplete experience, we complete the cube by 'appending' the other three sides. Bordwell and other cognitive film theorists argue that film is like a six-sided cube in which spectators see at most only three sides on screen. The spectator has to complete the film by appending the other three sides, so to speak" (Elsaesser and Buckland 2002: 170). Spectators enter the story world of a film with an internalized set of expectations, and when presented with two or more events in a film, they link these events "either spatially, temporally, and/or causally" (Elsaesser and Buckland 2002: 171). Spectators analyze films through schemata, "norms and principles in the mind that organize the incomplete data into coherent mental representations, [and which] are activated by cues in the data" (Elsaesser and Buckland 2002: 170). Gaps in a film cue spectators to missing details, which they must then work to complete. The spectator generates a hypothesis or multiple hypotheses on the basis of these clues as well as from their knowledge of stories, which are expected to follow a predictable pattern of exposition: "the introduction of setting and characters—explanation of a state of affairs—complicating action—ensuing events—outcome—ending" (Bordwell 1985: 35). Filmmakers construct their films with an understanding of the ways in which spectators will make meaning from the information presented.

Bordwell uses the Russian formalist distinction between "story" (*fabula*) and "plot" (*syuzhet*) to describe the difference between the way a film presents material and the way this material is arranged into a narrative. A "plot" is the arrangement of the events in the order they are presented, which the spectator must arrange into the "story," the coherent, linear arrangement of the events in a cause-effect relationship. The story, however, is in a constant state of change (in the mind of the spectator) as a result of changing hypotheses in the ongoing process of film viewing. A major element of film style revolves around the structure of the plot. The classical style is characterized by its carefully measured presentation of narrative information and ultimate resolution of enigmas. Art cinema, by contrast, is often characterized by its inscrutability and lack of resolution: time and space are often fragmented and causality far from clear; in addition, characters may have traits that are not clearly defined or even contradictory. In short, any or all of the conventions of the classical style may be inverted in art cinema. The subjective realist multiform films that will be the focus of the coming chapters have characteristics of both of these styles. The temporal, spatial, causal, and ontological dimensions of these films are often fragmented and require more effort than usual to arrange into coherent stories. However, it will be argued that they *can* ultimately be arranged into coherent stories, and in this sense, they resemble their classical counterparts.

Fragmented Narratives

Geoff King begins his analysis of independent cinema narration with a consideration of what he calls "fragmented narrative." Fragmented narratives are defined by King as being decentered, lacking the types of strongly unified, forward-moving narrative of classical cinema. They feature "more relaxed or fragmented structures akin to those associated with some forms of international art cinema" (King 2005: 59). His examples include

Harmony Korine's *Gummo* (1997) and *Julien Donkey-Boy* (1999); Jim Jarmusch's *Stranger than Paradise* (1984), *Down by Law* (1986), and *Night on Earth* (1991); P.T. Anderson's *Hard Eight* (1997); Billy Bob Thornton's *Sling Blade* (1996); and Wes Anderson's *Bottle Rocket* (1996) (King 2005: 59). "Fragmentation," the way King uses it here, bears a close resemblance to what I would call episodic narrative structures. They feature loose causal chains, multiple protagonists, and more open narratives than Hollywood films, and in these ways, might be said to resemble episodic television. In addition to these examples, however, there are a number of other kinds of films that employ forms of fragmentation that are not considered by King under this rubric, but that seem to me to clearly warrant the label fragmented. Consequently, I want to expand the use of the term to include a number of techniques that indeed "fragment" the causal, temporal, or spatial conventions of the classical style. For instance: nonlinear plot structures; character motivation that is complex or unclear; or editing techniques used to disrupt causal and spatial dimensions of a narrative. Central to my argument, however, is that there is yet another type in addition to these that I will call ontological fragmentation.

Ontological fragmentation is a central feature of many subjective realist multiform films and results from unmarked shifts from one level of reality to another—from dreams to waking states, for instance. Changes in ontology are a common feature of many genres, with the dream sequence being the most common example of these types of shifts. Dream sequences, however, are usually clearly marked. At the end of a dream, for instance, the dreamer is shown waking. Other markers used for dreams and subjective sequences such as hallucinations or flashbacks are soft-focus photography, distorted décor, slow-motion cinematography, and slurred sound (Bordwell 2006: 15). In the classical Hollywood style, where the emphasis is on coherence, these markers are used in the service of keeping different levels of reality clearly demarcated. The type of shift that produces what I am calling ontological fragmentation, however, is one that is either not marked or not clearly marked. In *Mulholland Drive*, for instance, there are several ontological shifts that are not obvious and so create challenges for the spectator, whose attempts to assemble a story are complicated as a result. Indeed, many spectators and critics have concluded that *Mulholland Drive* is incomprehensible, and intentionally so. I will argue below that if *Mulholland Drive*'s ontological shifts are identified, a strong case can be made for a coherent reading. Unmarked ontological shifts such as those found in *Mulholland Drive* are a regular feature of the subjective realist multiform film, and the ontological fragmentation they cause is a recurring, if not definitive, trait of subjective realist multiform cinema.

Returning now to the narratives of American independent cinema, I want to briefly consider the question of *why* fragmented narratives are used in these films. Maybe not surprisingly, King tells us that fragmentation is often justified on the grounds that it offers a more accurate or authentic representation of the existential reality of the characters portrayed than a coherent, linear narrative would. For instance, in films such as *Gummo* and *Julien Donkey-Boy*, King sees a logic in the rejection of a unified narrative: *Gummo*'s fragmented narrative reflects the fragmentation of the impoverished and marginalized community depicted; and in *Julien*, fragmentation is used to represent the central character's deteriorating psyche. So, in contrast to the clearly motivated and clearly defined characters of classic narrative, characters in independent cinema sometimes have more ambiguous motivations. This departure is based, at least in part, on the filmmakers' desire to create a more authentic set of motivations, arguably more in line with the lives of the types of individuals being represented.

The idea that fragmented narrative forms are more authentic representations of the real is a theme that appears regularly in the discourse of alternative film, and it will be considered further in chapter 3, which explores the subjective realist mode of narration. Fragmented narratives are one of many techniques used to place spectators in a similarly troubled epistemological relationship to the diegetic world of the film as that of the central character. A key feature of subjective realist multiform films, from *Caligari* to *Eternal Sunshine*, then, is the use of a fragmented narrative. This fragmentation is always ontological, but very often it is temporal and spatial as well.

Multi-strand Narratives

The second common type of narrative employed in American independent cinema according to King is the multi-strand, a term he uses to identify films with more than one narrative or those that follow more than one protagonist. (In fact, María del Mar Azcona's book *The Multi-Protagonist Film* [2010] considers a number of the same films identified by King, but emphasizes characters rather than just number of narrative strands.) The films of Robert Altman provide well-known examples of this style of narration, and films such as *Crash* (Paul Haggis 2004), *Babel*, and *Syriana* have employed multi-stranded structures to tell their stories as well. Multi-strand narratives are sometimes considered in their relationship to the episodic forms of television (as are some of the fragmented narratives of the films mentioned above). There are, however, examples of multi-strand films that predate the advent of television, such as Roberto Rossellini's *Paisà* (1946), which Bazin sees as "unquestionably the first film to resemble a collection of short stories" (1967: 34).

Several common types of multi-strand narratives have been identified, including the integrated, the separated, and the complex (Hassler-Forest 2006: n.p.). In the first style, there are varying degrees of integration among the different strands of the story. This may be partial—as in Altman's *Short Cuts* (1993), where narrative overlap is tangential to the individual stories—or more full, as in *Magnolia* and *Happiness* (Todd Solondz 1997), where the overlap is more crucial to both the overarching and individual stories (King 2005: 88). In both *Magnolia* and *Happiness*, for instance, there are several narrative strands, each of which follows different protagonists whose actions are interconnected in important ways to the story. In multi-strand narratives that are separated, by contrast, various formal devices may be used to link the distinct narrative strands. Jim Jarmusch's *Mystery Train* (1989), for instance, features several such devices. First, the three stories are set in the same location—downtown Memphis—and further, the stories take place simultaneously, though they are presented sequentially. Next, a gunshot that takes place in the first strand is overheard by characters in the second and third. The gunshot serves as a temporal marker of the overlap in each strand and the common setting establishes the spatial relationship between them. Hal Hartley's *Flirt* (1995) uses a slightly different formal device for unifying its strands: it features four vignettes that repeat the same narrative scenario and dialogue using different actors in different cities across the globe. In *Flirt*, it is the repetition of narrative material that unifies the film's multiple strands. So, while *Mystery Train*'s characters are connected by spatial proximity, in *Flirt*, there is no such connection. Dan Hassler-Forest's article "Multiple Narrative Structures" (2006) presents a simple system of classification for the numerous types of narratives with examples of multi-strand films dating back to *Intolerance* (D.W. Griffith 1916).

Forest's categories are useful, particularly his characterization of complex multiple narrative structure, which he describes as a structure with four or more strands unified by tightly defined formal parameters of time and/or space.[10] These formal parameters are used to prevent a breakdown of comprehension on the part of spectators, and Robert Altman's films *Nashville* (1975), *Short Cuts* (1993), and *Gosford Park* (2001), as well as Anderson's *Magnolia*, are examples of the complex multiple narrative films. King, in his analysis of *Magnolia* and *Happiness*, argues that if the typical Hollywood narrative is like a short story, these complex multi-strand films—which often feature themes of loneliness and isolation and attempts by the characters to make connections with others—are more novelistic, "relatively closer to the dense complexity of real life" (King 2005: 91). In terms of complexity, when multi-strand narratives are combined with other aesthetic techniques, even more challenging narrative spaces may be created. For example, Iñárritu's *Amores Perros* (2000), *21 Grams* (2003), and *Babel* all feature not only multi-strand narratives, but also fragmented temporalities.

The use of multi-strand narration in the early years of the twenty-first century is notable to film critics like David Denby because it has been put to use in these big-budget productions with ensemble casts featuring Brad Pitt and Cate Blanchett (*Babel*) or George Clooney and Matt Damon (*Syriana*) and marketed not to the audiences of Robert Altman, Jim Jarmusch, or Hal Hartley, but to the global multiplex audiences of *Pulp Fiction* and *The English Patient*. That these films have reached these audiences is possibly what is most surprising for critics since their multiple strands make for a rather complex cinematic experience—a pleasure, Denby notes, formerly reserved for much smaller audiences. Ultimately, however, these films do not push the limits of comprehension very far. They cannot. There is too much at stake financially and the producers and filmmakers know they must walk the fine line between experimentation and conventionality. There is, however, a class of films that have pushed these boundaries slightly further, and near the end of his analysis of multi-strand narrative, King introduces some of these films. They feature what he describes as a more "radical toying with different threads, and with the basis of narrative structure as a whole" (2005: 98). King mentions both *Memento* and *Mulholland Drive* as examples, recognizing their distinctiveness from the multi-strand; yet, he offers little in the way of analysis. He is content to offer a list of films with narratives that do not quite fit his categories, describe some of their narrative characteristics, and leave it at that. It is here, then, at the outer reaches of the multi-strand narrative that the limitations of King's attempt to categorize narrative forms becomes evident. It is also here that the distinction between the multi-strand and the multiform becomes crucial.

Multiform Narratives

Multiform narratives are related to but distinct from multi-strand narratives. What relates them is the shared feature of two or more narrative strands, a similarity that has led critics such as Denby and scholars such as King to group the styles together. What the multiform offers as a category, however, is a way of conceptualizing and articulating their difference: the multiplicity of the multiform is not simply narratological but also ontological—it features parallel or alternate realities in one or more of its strands. Multiform narratives are common in science fiction, horror, and fantasy films with examples ranging from *The Matrix* to *The Wizard of Oz* (Victor Fleming 1939) to *A Nightmare on Elm Street* (Wes Craven 1984). However, they have also been a mainstay of international art cinema, where they have been used to represent the subjective perspectives of unstable characters for nearly a century. Examples from this stream include Robert Weine's *The Cabinet of Dr. Caligari*, Ingmar Bergman's *Wild Strawberries*, as well as Federico Fellini's *8½* to name but a few. In films such as *Mulholland Drive*, *Memento*, and *Eternal Sunshine*, subjective realist multiform narratives are similarly employed to represent the subjective perspective of their central characters, where the alternate realities represented include, among other things, hallucinations, memories, dreams, and/or psychotic states. What I will do now is survey the extremely limited discourse around multiform cinema in order to, first, build a richer working definition of the term than has been provided thus far, and, second, to situate my argument in relation to this work.

The use of the term "multiform" to describe narratives with multiple ontological levels originates with Janet H. Murray, whose *Hamlet on the Holodeck* (1997) considers the roots of multiform narrative in literature, as well as exploring examples from film and television. She writes, "I am using the term *multiform story* to describe a written or dramatic narrative that presents a single situation or plotline in multiple versions, versions that would be mutually exclusive in our ordinary experience" (1997: 30). It is the "mutual exclusivity" of the versions that provides the key to Murray's notion of the multiform. Murray's coining of "multiform narrative" seems to have resulted from the absence of a narratological vocabulary with which to articulate the types of narratives she has seen developing in the hypertextual cyberspace stories her book focuses on. What Murray does not do, however, is argue that multiform narrative is a new phenomenon, and her examples make this clear. She considers Frank Capra's *It's a Wonderful Life* (1946), Robert Zemeckis's *Back to the Future* (1985), and Harold Ramis's *Groundhog Day* (1993), and shows that each features narrative strands that present mutually exclusive or alternate realities: the first supernatural, the next futuristic, and the last, unexplained—possibly supernatural, possibly delusional. The examples I have cited from do not feature in Murray's analysis, although she does consider the Japanese classic *Rashomon* in her analysis of a subtype of the multiform that she calls the "violence-hub narrative" (1997: 135).

Violence-hub narratives, according to Murray, "place an account of a violent incident . . . at the center of a web of narratives that explore it from multiple points of view" (1997: 137).[11] *Rashomon* serves as the quintessential cinematic example of the type. "These violence-hub stories do not have a single solution like the adventure maze or a refusal of solution like postmodern stories; instead, they combine a clear sense of story structure with a multiplicity of meaningful plots. The navigation of the labyrinth is like pacing the floor; a physical manifestation of the effort to come to terms with the trauma, it represents the mind's repeated efforts to keep returning to a shocking event in an effort to absorb it and, finally, get past it" (1997: 135–36). Violence-hub narratives also exploit the potential of the multiform to represent the pathological subjectivities that often result from trauma, a theme that will be considered further in chapter 5. The violence-hub form of the multiform narrative is an important category here because it is the one most commonly used in the subjective realist multiform cinema.

Another common type of multiform narrative, treated by Murray but not named, is what David Bordwell has referred to as the "forking-path narrative." Forking-path films use multiform structures to represent the multiple possible futures of their central characters. Bordwell's article, "Film Futures" (2003), begins with reference to the short story written by Jorge Luis Borges, "The Garden of Forking Paths" (first published in 1941), which is often cited by theorists dealing with multiform narratives. In Borges's short story, the notion of the forking path is based on a (nonexistent) novel in which a man who, faced with a choice between a diverse set of alternative futures, chooses them all simultaneously. The novel is described by Borges as following the man through each of those alternate worlds, and at every point in each of these alternate narratives, when he is faced with a choice, the novel fragments and follows him; and so on, ad infinitum. Obviously, a novel of this sort is impossible, and, Bordwell observes, so would a film be. He argues that cinematic forking-path narratives are even more limited than their literary cousins, and in the films he considers, the infinite possibilities stipulated by Borges generally narrow to around three (fairly similar) possible alternate worlds.[12] His examples are *Blind Chance* (Krzysztof Kieslowski 1981), *Too Many Ways to be Number One* (Wai Ka-Fai 1997), *Run Lola Run* (Tom Tykwer 1998), and *Sliding Doors* (Peter Howitt 1998). Each of these films features a forking-path structure with a maximum of three and minimum of two alternate futures. Most present the alternate futures serially, but one—*Sliding Doors*—presents its two narratives through crosscutting. Bordwell's examples confirm his thesis that forking-path narratives are not actually complex after all, since apart from their multiple strands representing multiple possibilities, the films generally conform to rules of classical narration. Edward Branigan, in a response to Bordwell's article, has proposed the term be used "as a way of marking a conservative, generic form of narrative" ("Nearly

True" 2002: 108). Forking-path narratives can be understood as a subcategory or type of multiform film. Like the multiform narratives of science fiction and fantasy films, what distinguishes them from the subjective realist multiform film is their less-than-naturalistic premises.

In contrast to forking-path narratives, the films I will consider have more naturalistic premises, and Murray's notion of the violence-hub narrative becomes a useful point of reference here. The alternate realities they explore are set in the minds of the characters seeking to come to grips with trauma; consequently, their multiple realities are realistic in the sense that they depict experiences that, although not common, do occur with some regularity. *Rashomon*, for instance, explores a murder via a series of what-if scenarios as imagined by a group of characters seeking to make sense of the event. Three of the films I will consider below, *Mulholland Drive*, *Memento*, and *Eternal Sunshine*, offer variations on the violence-hub structure as well. Consequently, Murray's work provides a way to articulate similarities in the multiform films I am analyzing: each features a traumatic event as its central causal feature. The event and its effects also motivate the use of an ontologically fragmented narrative structure. In *Mulholland Drive* and *Memento* it is the death or murder of a lover—and in *Eternal Sunshine*, it is the breakup of a relationship. The use of trauma as a central causal feature can also be argued to operate in classic examples of the subjective realist multiform films like *The Cabinet of Dr. Caligari*, *Wild Strawberries*, *Persona*, and *8½*.

Ruth Perlmutter has explored the connection between trauma and multiform narrative in her article "Memories, Dreams, Screens," which examines a group of films—including *Mulholland Drive* and *Memento*—focusing primarily on how the narratives are used to represent characters trapped in traumatic repetition:

> The films that concern me here . . . make use of dreams and memories to express the tension between remembering and repressing an unacceptable past. The repression often takes a neuro-pathological form, in that the films tend to be driven by characters with either hysterical transference (such as an exchange of personalities) or a psychological ailment—amnesia, muteness, paralysis. They hide behind these psychic maladies in an effort to seek a new identity or escape into alternative selves (a desire that often gets expressed by serialization—successive what-if scenarios, parallel worlds, multiple outcome narratives). (2005: 125)

Perlmutter's article, though it does not use the term "multiform narrative" or "violence-hub narrative," focuses almost exclusively on films that use these forms to represent the effects of trauma on subjectivity. Her organizing concept is the "trance film," which is a term often used to describe the experimental films of Maya Deren, which are notable for their exploration of trauma. What Perlmutter's article makes clear is that fragmented structures and mixed ontologies—forms common to international art cinema and the contemporary American independent cinema that borrows from it—are very well suited for representing the fractured forms of consciousness that are often associated with trauma. As a result, her work will be used in several of the chapters that follow.

In a slightly different vein, Alison McMahan's article "The Effect of Multiform Narrative on Subjectivity" provides one of the few instances of film scholarship that has actually employed Murray's concept. McMahan's article examines multiform narrative in Hollywood cinema in order to demonstrate how it has "absorbed the lessons of multiform subjectivity in interactive media and applied it to the more linear cinema" (1999: 146). McMahan cites Terry Gilliam's *12 Monkeys* (1995) as an example of a film that features three plots and three parallel worlds: the future, where the narrative begins; the past, depicted via the fragmented dreams of Cole (Bruce Willis); and the present, represented through four instances of time travel. McMahan notes that in *12 Monkeys*—as in most Hollywood films with parallel plot structures—all the plot lines converge in one climax, "providing the closure required by linear form" (1999: 148). She adds, "multiform plots are basically several linear plots loosely knitted together; each separate strand still follows the classic rules of causal transformation" (1999: 148). Her description of multiform narrative resembles King's description of the multi-strand narrative and Bordwell's of forking-path films, yet her key example, *12 Monkeys*, features elements that, although not articulated, are constitutive of multiform narrative as it will be used here. These are dual- or multi-strand narratives with two or more ontologies. McMahan concludes her article by predicting that "multiform plots and multiform characters will migrate from the horror, science-fiction, and fantasy genres to other genres," a prediction that has, in fact, already come to pass,[13] and one that N. Katherine Hayles and Nicholas Gessler have examined in their work on multiform cinema (1999: 156–57).

Hayles and Gessler explore what they call "slipstream" fiction, defined as "works that occupy a borderland between mainstream and science fiction because they achieve a science-fictional feeling without the usual defamiliarization devices" (2004: 482). Their examples include *The Thirteenth Floor* (Joseph Rusnak 1999), *Dark City* (Alex Proyas 1998), and *Mulholland Drive*, films that they argue challenge everyday notions of reality and foreground ontological issues in much the same way as science fiction narratives do, yet, are not science fiction.[14] Hayles and Gessler argue that *Mulholland Drive* unsettles spectators' ontological security through its creation of a "mixed reality," which is done through its dream sequences, hallucinations, and flashbacks. Since the film does not establish a normative ontological framework before introducing the dream world (as many feature films do), *Mulholland Drive* complicates the viewer's ability to distinguish the real from the fantastic, oneiric, or hallucinatory. Unlike McMahan's description, the idea of "mixed ontology" is a clearly articulated characteristic of multiform narrative for Hayles and Gessler. Their work is important here not only because it is, along with McMahan's work, among the only applications of Murray's term to cinema, but also because of the important distinction they make between the multiform narratives of science fiction and those of what they call slipstream fiction. Science fiction grounds its alternate realities in a material explanation, usually a futuristic technology, whereas slipstream fiction employs subjective realism. *12 Monkeys* offers multiple alternate realities, for instance. One is the result of a time machine used by James Cole to travel back in time, but there are a number of others that represent a recurring dream of Cole's in which he sees slightly different versions of his own death. The subjective realist multiform narrative of Terry Gilliam's earlier multiform film *Brazil* (1985), although also set in the future, is a result not of time travel but of the fantasy world of its central character. As in Gilliam's *The Fisher King* (1991), the representation of the central character's madness is the motivating force behind the use of the multiform narrative. As it also uses a multiform narrative to represent the subjective reality of its central character, it is an example of the type of multiform film I want to explore here. I want to take time now, then, to illustrate how this works.

Brazil

Brazil can be described as a black, science fiction comedy set in a futuristic Orwellian bureaucratic-fascist dystopia. It uses a multiform narrative to represent the increasingly delusional reality of its central character, Sam Lowery (Jonathan Pryce), a highly capable but extremely unmotivated civil servant working in the Ministry of Information. Lowery is introduced to spectators via a dream sequence (the first of the film's two subjective realist strands) in which he appears as a kind of medieval superhero, flying above the clouds by means of mechanical wings attached to his suit of armor. The ontological status of the scene, which is actually a dream, is not signaled until its conclusion, when Sam is summoned back to the waking world by a phone call from his incompetent boss, Mr. Kurtzman

(Ian Holm). The ambiguity of the scene results, in part, from its visual contrast to the grim steampunk interiors of the film's earlier scenes, and its ontological departure foreshadows Sam's own progressive disconnection from this world. Sam's dream is recurring and serves as one of the film's three key narratives.

The first and primary strand of *Brazil* features a love story between Sam and Jill Layton (Kim Greist), whom he meets when he is sent to sort out a case of mistaken identity that has led to the accidental death in captivity of an innocent man, Layton's neighbor, Archibald Buttle. Much of the action in this strand follows Sam as he pursues Layton, but there is also a subplot that features Robert De Niro as the plumber-terrorist Archibald *Tuttle*,[15] who assists Sam in his battle with the pedantic maintenance man Spoor (Bob Hoskins). The second and third narrative strands are both subjective realist; that is, they both represent Sam's dreams and fantasies from his perspective. The first of these follows the ongoing dream in which Sam features as the superhero-like warrior who battles the forces of evil in order to free captives and rescue a beautiful maiden, and it follows a similar trajectory to the romance but in fragments that interrupt the main narrative. The second subjective realist strand represents a delusional escape fantasy that takes place during Sam's state-sponsored torture in "The Ministry of Information Retrieval" near the end of the film. It presents Sam's imaginary rescue by Tuttle and a band of armed terrorists. Since the shift that leads into this strand is unmarked, spectators assume that the events it depicts are taking place on the same level as previous events. However, there are instances of spatial, temporal, and causal disruptions that ultimately point to its status as fantasy. These disruptions include the reappearance of a building after its demolition, doorways that lead impossibly from one place to another, and the unexplained reappearance of a character who has died in an earlier scene. These types of disruptions are eventually given an explanation when the sequence ends and the narration returns to Sam in the torture chamber at the Ministry of Information Retrieval. It is at this point that it becomes clear that there has been an ontological shift, and that Sam's escape was fictional, a figment of his overwrought imagination. *Brazil* is a complex film that employs a multiform narrative to tell the story of a character experiencing a psychological breakdown. It uses a combination of aesthetic and narrative techniques that include a multi-stranded narrative, ontological fragmentation, and subjective realist narration. As such, it is a clear example of subjective realist multiform cinema, and in this brief analysis, I have sought to highlight some of the important features of multiform narrative as they will be explored in this book.

Puzzle Films

Before concluding this chapter, I want to consider some other work on what I am referring to as multiform cinema. This work has taken place under the very simple and useful heading of "complex narrative," which has come to be used to describe a wide spectrum of unconventional narrative styles used in the cinema. Warren Buckland's *Puzzle Films* has brought together the work of a number of different scholars in a collection of articles on complex narrative in contemporary cinema, several of which directly address the three key multiform films which serve as my own case studies. Buckland writes in his introduction: "The papers in this volume demonstrate that puzzle films embrace non-linearity, time loops, and fragmented spatio-temporal reality. These films blur the boundaries between different levels of reality, are riddled with gaps, deception, labyrinthine structures, ambiguity, and overt coincidences. They are populated with characters who are schizophrenic, lose their memory, are unreliable narrators, or are dead (but without them—or us—realizing)" (2009: 9). His description of "puzzle films" clearly includes the key characteristics of subjective multiform cinema as I have described it, particularly the notion of blurred "boundaries between different levels of reality."[16] Indeed, several of the many different categories employed by the book's authors are inclusive of the multiform narrative. Or, to be more specific, multiform films are cited as examples of many of the book's key categories, for instance: puzzle films, mind-game films, multiple-draft films, and twist films. Sometimes these terms are used interchangeably, as in Buckland's introduction, while at others, they are employed more specifically. Thomas Elsaesser's "mind-game film" is one of the most comprehensive of these categories and his chapter includes a survey of the narrative strategies employed in a huge range of complex films from the past and present. The mind-game film, according to Elsaesser, plays "mind games" at two levels: the character level and/or the audience level. He provides a number of examples of the first type, including David Fincher's *Se7en* (1995), in which "John Doe is playing games with the rookie policeman played by Brad Pitt" (Elsaesser 2009: 2). Other examples in which characters are the victims of games include *The Truman Show* (Peter Weir 1998) and *The Game* (David Fincher 1997).

In the second type of mind-game film, it is the spectators who are the victims of game playing, and both *Mulholland Drive* and *Memento* are included as examples. Mind games of this type result from crucial information being "withheld or ambiguously presented" (Elsaesser 2009: 2). If this crucial information is withheld from characters as well as from spectators, as it is in *Fight Club* (David Fincher 1999) and *The Sixth Sense* (M.

Night Shyamalan 1999), the presentation of the information strikes both characters and audiences as a revelation (thus, the "twist" of the twist film). *Memento* and *Eternal Sunshine* both employ such twists, and both use unmarked ontological shifts to create them. A further feature of some of the latter type of mind-game films according to Elsaesser are characters "whose mental condition is extreme, unstable, or pathological" but whose perspective "is presented as normal" (2009: 3). The withholding of crucial information and the presentation of extreme mental conditions are two of the key characteristics of the subjective realist multiform films under consideration here, and so, in relation to Elsaesser's work, this book could be considered to be an in-depth analysis of several examples from his second category of mind-game film. Here again, the "multiform" seems to offer a way of refining the categories presently used to refer to these complex films.

Buckland's book should be read as offering a point of contrast to the work of David Bordwell, who argues that complex structures often hide classical stories. To make his argument, Bordwell must, of course, ignore those aspects of the films he studies that do not fit the classical narrative structure, like the nonclassical nature of a character such as *Memento*'s Leonard Shelby (Guy Pearce). Buckland, by contrast, picks up exactly these aspects that do not fit and argues that these films do indeed represent something new, something that is not classical at all. To make his point, Buckland considers Aristotle's distinction between simple and complex plots and argues that the complexity of the puzzle film "far exceeds" Aristotle's notion of complexity. By this, Buckland means that these films are both complicated and perplexing. That is to say they are not necessarily unified, accessible, or even comprehensible. It seems indisputable that the plotting of many of the films considered "complex" breaks with the coherent linearity of the classical narrative. They have also been created with radical differences in perspective on mimesis to that of Aristotle, and if Bordwell's goal is to claim complex narrative for Aristotle, and Buckland's is to argue they are entirely new, the goal of this book is to do something related to but different from both. It does not argue for the "classical" nature of the contemporary cycle of complex narrative cinema, but rather for a recognition of the influence of the cinema of the past on contemporary complex narrative cinema. At the same time, while digital technologies may well have influenced the production and reception of films like *Eternal Sunshine* and *Inception*, it is also accurate to say that their debt to the surrealism of Buñuel and Dalí is profound. Further, the influence on Hollywood of art cinema, experimental cinema, independent cinema, and the national cinema and various film movements from around the globe is undeniable, as the examples in this book will demonstrate.

My argument is not that films such as *Memento* or *Eternal Sunshine* are classical in an Aristotelian sense (which is Bordwell's view, or at least the view that Buckland attributes to him), but rather that, regardless of their temporal, spatial, causal, and ontological fragmentation, narrative meaning can be made from the scattered constituents of their multiform plots. The subjective realist multiform films that are the subject of this book are considered for the manner in which they integrate experimental narrative styles into their stories, which in the end, do offer audiences a chain of events in a cause-and-effect relationship in space and time. A related argument emerging from this analysis is that, given the high cost of making, distributing, marketing, and exhibiting a feature film theatrically, narrative comprehensibility is a valued and valuable characteristic for audiences, and consequently, for producers as well. Complexity comes in degrees and it is often the case that box-office returns are closely tied to the level of comprehensibility of a narrative. This means that the commercial imperatives of narrative cinema greatly delimit the level of narrative complexity of the contemporary cinema.

Notes

1. I use the term "groundbreaking" here to indicate the unprecedented *commercial* success of *Pulp Fiction*.
2. This trend has culminated, perhaps, in films such as *Inception*, the complex narrative blockbuster.
3. See Peter Biskind's *Down and Dirty Pictures* (2004), James Mottram's *The Sundance Kids: How the Mavericks Took Back Hollywood* (2006), and Alisa Perren's "Sex, Lies, and Marketing: Miramax and the Development of the Quality Indie Blockbuster" (2002).
4. *Eternal Sunshine* was produced by Focus Features (formerly October Films), a quasi-independent company owned by Universal. *Mulholland Drive* was financed by ABC TV, a subsidiary of Disney.
5. The circumstances of *Mulholland Drive*'s production make its hybridity unsurprising, as well as making the film an interesting example of the circuitous methods of production in the New Hollywood. *Mulholland Drive* was originally produced in 1999 as the pilot episode of a television series for the American Broadcasting Company (ABC). However, after forcing Lynch to shorten the extremely long first edition, executives from ABC were not convinced of its viability and declined to air it (Buckland 2003: 133). After a brief hiatus, the project was revived in 2000 when it was purchased by Les Films Alain Sarde (owned by Le Canal Plus) for the seven million dollars ABC had invested in it. Lynch was given additional funding to convert the pilot into a feature film (Buckland 2003: 133); it is said that he received an additional seven million dollars, and if this is the case, *Mulholland Drive* was produced at costs (fourteen million dollars) well below the average of a Hollywood film of the time (estimated at about forty million dollars (Weintraub 1997: n.p.)). *Mulholland Drive*, then, was produced with funding from both a major studio and a

large European entertainment corporation on a budget of less than half the industry average.
6. Bordwell, in writing about *Memento* and *Eternal Sunshine* in *The Way Hollywood Tells It* (2006), simply treats them as Hollywood films.
7. Particularly in Geoff King's taxonomy.
8. I add "partially" because the gap is a large one and the category of multiform only addresses a small part of this gap.
9. The use of the term "art cinema" often represents an attempt to group many disparate films together under one convenient rubric and minimizes differences between the individual films or movements it is used to refer to. The term is, then, somewhat reductive. Yet, just as a general description of the narrational strategies of the "classical Hollywood style" can help us understand how many films are constructed and why, so a general description of "art cinema" narration can contribute to an understanding of certain types of films made outside Hollywood.
10. Rick Altman's *A Theory of Narrative* (2008) similarly identifies what he calls single-focus, dual-focus, and multiple-focus narratives.
11. What is notable about multiform narrative in contemporary cinema is not its novelty, then, but the frequency with which it is used: multiform narratives appear in science fiction and horror films on a regular basis; there have been a number of big-budget Hollywood films that have used them; and, of course, they often appear in independent features. There is, consequently, a clear need for explorations of multiform films in these genres, and the type of analysis required is well beyond the scope of the book. My choice of films from the American independent context is partially the result of personal taste; however, in tracing the origins of multiform cinema, it is clear that its roots are firmly in the art cinema tradition and the independent mode of filmmaking is often seen as an extension of that tradition.
12. Each of Bordwell's examples features a forking-path structure with a maximum of three and minimum of two alternate futures. He writes:

> None of these films hints at the radical possibilities opened by Borges [and] none of these plots confronts the ultimate Borgesian demands . . . we have something far simpler, corresponding to a more cognitively manageable conception of what forking paths would be like in our own lives. Far from representing a failure of nerve on the part of film directors, I think that this tendency offers clues to the way forking-path narratives actually work and work upon us . . . Storytellers' well-entrenched strategies for manipulating time, space, causality, point of view, and all the rest reflect what is perceptually and cognitively manageable for their audiences, and the multiple worlds of Borges and quantum mechanics don't fit that condition. Add to this the canons and conventions of the medium as well, and these may work to limit the proliferation of forking paths. (Bordwell 2003: 89–91)

The stated purpose of Bordwell's article is to "chart some of the key conventions" of the forking-path films he considers, conventions which, the reader discovers, are primarily ones that limit the infinite possibilities of the form to produce cognitively manageable versions. Indeed, part of the pleasure of these films stems from their reintroduction of "viewer-friendly devices in the context of what might seem to be ontologically or epistemically radical possibilities" (Bordwell 2003: 91). Bordwell's examples, and his conclusions, have led scholars like Edward Branigan to see the forking-path film as "a conservative, generic form of narrative" (2002: 112). Jan Simons summarizes the article this way: "Forking-path narratives, then, may push the envelope, but on closer analysis they turn out not to be complex at all" (2008: 112). From the perspective of my argument, Bordwell's forking-path narrative is a type of multiform film, but, like the science fiction and fantasy multiform films that his examples most resemble, require some type of supernatural explanation for their forms (e.g., they are fantastic-marvelous). They are not subjective realist but closer to fantasy.

13. Of course, this prediction is quite belated since early instances of its use in the predicted manner date back to at least the 1940s. McMahan's article, like Murray's book, is also notable for its absence of any reference to the use of multiform narrative in the art cinema, a surprising omission given its publication in such a high-profile journal as *Screen*.

14. According to Adam Roberts, science fiction "requires a material, physical rationalization, rather than a supernatural or arbitrary one . . . this grounding of Science Fiction in the material rather than the supernatural becomes one of its key features" (2000: 5). The idea of the supernatural will be discussed later in relation to Todorov's distinction between the uncanny and the marvelous; however, I would contend that both *The Thirteenth Floor* and *Dark City* are clear examples of science fiction films.

15. The mistaken arrest of Buttle is the result of a clerical error, and it is actually Tuttle the authorities are after.

16. Buckland mentions two key factors in his description of the "puzzle film" (which for all intents and purposes, seems to be identical to Elasesser's "mind-game film" [see below]). First he identifies the narrative characteristics and then he describes the context from which these films emerge. I will quote him at length:

> In the end, the complexity of puzzle films operates on two levels: narrative and narration. It emphasizes the complex *telling* (plot, narration) of a simple or complex *story* (narrative). The term "puzzle film" names a mode of filmmaking that cuts across traditional filmmaking practices, all of which are becoming increasingly difficult to define: so-called American "independent" cinema, the European and International Art film, and certain modes of avant-garde filmmaking. Rather than try to redefine these practices, this volume unites them on the basis of their shared storytelling complexity. This "unity" is of course outweighed by the diversity of each film. (2009: 9)

> Puzzle films, in this description, are simply films with complex narratives, where "complex" is used to distinguish these films from classical forms. Buckland's distinction is rooted in the ongoing debate over classical and postclassical filmmaking considered above and is the counterargument to what is seen as Bordwell's reduction of these films into classical terms. For my purposes, what is important here is the way in which "puzzle film" is used: it is a broad term that includes multiform and subjective realist multiform films as I have described them. Buckland's term overlaps considerably with Elsaesser's "mind-game," and he writes: "Indeed, we could argue that the puzzle film is the mind-game seen from one theoretical perspective—narratology" (Buckland 2009: 12).

Chapter 2

TWO TRAJECTORIES OF THE CINEMA OF ATTRACTIONS

The story of early cinema has often been considered as an evolution from its primitive theatrical stage to a higher and more refined stage of narrative expression. Tom Gunning, however, has challenged this view in an argument that unites prenarrative film "in a conception that sees cinema less as a way of telling stories than as a way of presenting a series of views to an audience" (1990: 57). He argues that before 1906, early cinema, in both its actuality and nonactuality modes, was characterized by a presentational style. The Lumière brothers' actuality films depicted simple scenes from everyday life and were astounding for their audiences simply as a result of their novelty: their ability to convey the photographic illusion of motion. This is evident when one considers the mythology surrounding the premiere of *The Arrival of a Train at La Ciotat Station* (1895), for example, during which the audience supposedly fled in fear of an actual train. On the other hand, Méliès's nonactuality films used the new medium in ways that exploited its ability to convey the illusion of magic, using stop-action photography and special effects to create trick films such as *The Vanishing Lady* (1896), or elaborately staged fantasies like *A Trip to the Moon* (1902) to amaze audiences. Gunning unites these styles of filmmaking under the heading of "the cinema of attractions." What distinguishes this "cinema of attractions" from the narrative cinema that followed it is the nature of its relationship with spectators, which Gunning describes as *exhibitionistic*. In the early cinema, direct address was common as performers in these films related to the camera in a similar way they would have to the audiences of the stage performances on which the films were based. Gunning illustrates this by way of an erotic film, *The Bride Retires* (France 1902), in which the bride performs a striptease for the camera, rather than for her husband, who is waiting behind a nearby curtain. In both the actuality and nonactuality forms, the "cinema of attractions" was fascinating for spectators not because of its narrative dimensions, which were lacking or even nonexistent, but because it offered audiences a new way of seeing the world, different from existing visual media like photography or painting. The cinema of attractions offered audiences the illusion of motion and magic and it offered filmmakers the ability to surprise and shock audiences in entirely new ways. However, when the novelty of the new medium began to fade, filmmakers began to develop techniques that elicited a more in-depth engagement with story instead. As narrative cinema developed, the continuity style quickly replaced the presentationalism of the cinema of attractions.

The continuity style that developed eschewed the overt exhibitionism of the early cinema, including its use of techniques such as direct address, because they were seen to interfere with the realistic diegetic space it sought to create. The goal of this new style was (and still is) the transformation of the screen into a transparent window through which spectators gaze into the story world of the film. In contrast to the exhibitionism of the cinema of attractions, then, narrative cinema is often described as voyeuristic: spectators watch characters who are seemingly unaware of being watched.[1] Although this exhibitionism/voyeurism dichotomy has proven to be a useful way of contrasting the cinema of attractions with narrative cinema by illustrating the difference in performance styles as well as their different effects on spectators, it is not an entirely accurate account, as Gunning himself acknowledges. There are two main problems with it: the first is the idea that narrative cinema displaced the cinema of attractions; and the second is the idea that a clear distinction can be made between the exhibitionism of the cinema of attractions and the voyeurism of narrative cinema, neither of which is wholly accurate.

Although the cinema of attractions has been replaced by narrative cinema as the dominant mode of filmmaking, from its beginnings, narrative cinema has maintained important elements of the cinema of attractions. There have always been films and even entire genres in which presentational or exhibitionistic aspects can be found. Gunning cites both musicals and chase films as a part of the "Méliès tradition," in which exhibitionistic aspects of the cinema of attractions are employed in Hollywood narrative films. Musicals employ direct address and bodily exhibitionism in similar ways to *The Bride Retires*, and early chase films offer the excitement of movement and spectacle comparable to that offered by *A Trip to the Moon*. Gunning further argues that a similar type of exhibitionism is still very much a part of contemporary Hollywood in "the Spielberg-Lucas-Coppola cinema of effects" (1990: 61). In so doing, he directly links the spectacle of the Hollywood blockbuster to the exhibitionism of cinema of attractions.

Gunning's work also identifies an avant-garde current of the cinema of attractions that "can be traced from Méliès through Keaton, through *Un Chien Andalou* (1928), and Jack Smith" (1990: 61). In this sense, there is also a clear relationship between avant-garde filmmakers like Buñuel, who employed cinematic techniques developed by Méliès to create their surrealist dreamscapes, and the contemporary films under consideration. Films such as *Mulholland Drive, Memento,* and *Eternal Sunshine* can be understood, in part, in terms of their relationship to this avant-garde current of filmmaking. Before looking more closely at this, however, I want to briefly explore the relationship between the cinema of attractions, classical Hollywood narration, and the blockbuster in order to examine how the mainstream trajectory has combined attractions with narrative forms to create a cinema that is both exhibitionistic and voyeuristic at the same time.

The Narrative Trajectory: Realism and Spectacle

David Bolter and Nicholas Grusin, in *Remediation,* argue that since at least the Renaissance, Western visual media "have sought immediacy through the interplay of the aesthetic value of transparency with the techniques of linear perspective, erasure, and automaticity" (2000: 24). In painting, for instance, the development of linear perspective, combined with more accurate techniques of rendering, allowed artists to "put the viewer in the same space as objects viewed," creating a new level of realism in representational art (2000: 11). Centuries later, the invention of photography would mark yet another step forward by achieving similar effects mechanically. Photography was hailed for its ability to produce the perfectly transparent window of representation, and it was seen to effectively remove subjectivity from the equation by eliminating the artist "as an agent who stood between the viewer and the reality of the image" (2000: 26). That there was excitement over the possibility of removing subjectivity provides insight as to why immediacy—and by extension, the realism based on transparency—has been so highly prized since the Renaissance. Realism was directly related to the epistemological project of the Enlightenment, which sought "immediacy" in the realm of knowledge (and realism in its art). In this sense, immediacy is tied to a correspondence theory of knowledge and the belief that the proper methodology—if found—would provide the subject with unmediated (immediate) access to reality. Philosophically, immediacy is about access to truth, whereas artistically, it is about verisimilitude, or the accurate representation of the real.[2] The realism of the classical Hollywood style is a product of this centuries-old project.

Bolter and Grusin cite *Strange Days* (Kathryn Bigelow 1995) as an example of a film that explores the idea of what a perfectly immediate technology might look like. *Strange Days*, set in the not-too-distant future, features a fictional technology referred to as "the wire," which enables the recording and playback of direct experience: it "bypasses all forms of mediation and transmits directly from one consciousness to another" (2000: 3).[3] As such, "the wire" immerses its user in an experience that erases the awareness of its mediated nature (much like the matrix does to the uninitiated in the *Matrix* trilogy). The experience offered by "the wire" is an example of the type of immediacy sought by realist art forms. Although the classical Hollywood style is no match for "the wire," its goals are similar. It offers a form of immediacy that immerses spectators in the diegetic world of a film. Indeed, Bolter and Grusin see the classical Hollywood style of narration as the filmic equivalent to linear perspective in painting, that is, as an attempt to erase evidence of mediation in an effort to produce transparent immediacy.[4]

As a general rule, the classical Hollywood style can be seen as an attempt to generate in spectators a sense of immediacy by eliciting absorption in the narrative. It hides its constructedness and rejects techniques that are seen to impede absorption. Indeed, it is the anti-realistic dimension of the spectacle that is often at the center of critiques leveled at contemporary forms of cinema such as the blockbuster. Thomas Schatz's criticism of the New Hollywood briefly introduced in chapter 1 can be seen as representative of one side of the debate over the matter, in which spectacle is viewed as disrupting narrative coherence to offer audiences low-brow thrills, not in service of the story, but for the pleasures they offer in and of themselves. Whether these are computer-generated dinosaurs and orcs or the erotic spectacle of the body, narrative coherence suffers in what is seen as the shift away from more narratively driven cinema of the past.[5]

The spectacle common to the blockbuster is often (though not exclusively) linked to new forms of technology, and the blockbuster has undeniably been the site for showcasing the potential of new forms such as computer-generated imagery or the capabilities of 7.1 sound systems, for instance. The use of technology in this manner is by no means a new phenomenon and one only need to look to the *The Jazz Singer* (Alan Crosland 1927) for parallels. More recent examples of technologically influenced spectacle such as that featured in *Avatar* (James Cameron 2009) have similar characteristics. What the *Jazz Singer* example makes clear, however, is that spectacle of this type is not a phenomenon limited to the blockbuster of the New Hollywood but one that has been a part of the appeal of narrative cinema from its earliest days (King 2002: 181). This fact often seems to be overlooked by critics such as Schatz, for whom the blockbuster has displaced the well-made story and spectacle has displaced narrative. In contrast to Schatz, David Bordwell maintains that the classical Hollywood style is still the dominant aesthetic mode in the New Hollywood and that classical narrative has not, in any significant way, been abandoned, even in the blockbuster. The debate on the matter is centered on the question of whether or not spectacle and narrative are mutually exclusive elements in the cinema and takes place within a larger context of what Thomas Elsaesser and Warren Buckland describe as the debate over classical and postclassical Hollywood aesthetics. Scholars like Elsaesser, Buckland, and Geoff King have demonstrated that spectacle and narrative are not mutually exclusive elements but often operate together, or at least side by side, and this seems to me to be the most persuasive position on the matter.

King, for instance, argues that a narrow view of "classical Hollywood narrative" compartmentalizes non-narrative or extranarrative dimensions "rather than allowing for the possibility that they might be just as much part of the essential fabric of classical-era Hollywood as the classical form of narrative structure" (2002: 182). King thinks that this opens the door for an ill-founded dismissal of the blockbuster as a radical departure from the aesthetic forms of the past, which he argues is simply not the case. He notes that when the "story-film" became dominant, narrative was often combined with "other pleasures" including chases, stunts, musical numbers, and spectacular scenery (2002: 182). In other words, he echoes Gunning's point regarding the manner in which the cinema of attractions is taken up by Hollywood, and argues that, although blockbusters do foreground spectacle, it does not follow that this results in the absence of narrative. King posits that the blockbuster generally has one of several different types of narratives—including but not limited to the classical narrative form—and he illustrates this with the example of *Terminator Two: Judgment Day* (James Cameron 1991), which, although a spectacular special-effects-driven film, also maintains many of the narrative elements of classical narrative: linear time sequencing, strong cause-effect relations, and clearly motivated characters who undergo significant development (2005: 122). King mentions other types of narratives common to the contemporary blockbuster such as the episodic narrative of television serials, as featured in *Raiders of the Lost Ark* (Steven Spielberg 1981): the fast-paced, action-centered spectacle-driven plots with shorter discursive segments; and others, which use fewer action sequences punctuated by longer discursive and character-oriented scenes (2005: 62–63). There are, of course, degrees of momentum and depth in these films, but King argues that considering narrative along these lines avoids the unfounded dismissal of the blockbuster on the grounds of its lack of narrative.

Buckland and Elsaesser present a reading of *Die Hard* (John McTiernan 1988) that illustrates the same point. Reading the film through both classical and postclassical critical frameworks, they conclude that the film can be seen to both follow the norms of canonical film narration and feature spectacle on a grand scale, demonstrating that the concepts are not mutually exclusive. They show that the debate results not so much from the difference between classic Hollywood film and contemporary blockbusters as from the theoretical frameworks used to analyze the films; so, after presenting a series of reviews critical of *Die Hard*'s narrative, Elsaesser and Buckland write: "One (polemical) way of defining the shift from the classical cinema to the post-classical is here encapsulated. It unfavorably contrasts the supposed absence of (narrative) substance with the fireworks of special effects, a roller coaster ride, which the critics nevertheless confess to being impressed by" (2002: 45). The debate is, they argue, generated not so much by a radical shift in emphasis—spectacle to the exclusion of narrative—as by the interpretations of films that the opposing theories produce. Spectacle is of central importance to the blockbuster, yet narrative is never entirely displaced. If we place these arguments in the context of the relationship between the blockbuster and the cinema of attractions, what can be said is that the blockbuster sits comfortably in the exhibitionistic tradition of filmmaking identified by Gunning. Yet, because the blockbuster is also largely narrative-driven and built on the classical style, it can be understood to be voyeuristic as well. The blockbuster, then, is both exhibitionistic and voyeuristic. It is not devoid of narrative, but employs different types of narratives in the service of spectacle. The arguments of King and others open a space in which the polarities of the debate over the blockbuster are less intense. It is evident that the blockbuster is not devoid of narrative and that it is possible for narrative and spectacle to work in conjunction with one another. With this said, however, it seems that a convincing argument can still be made that the narratives offered by blockbusters are often simplistic and predictable. For this reason, narrative is rarely, if ever, the key selling point of the blockbuster, which primarily relies on spectacle for both the pleasures it offers and its promotional appeal.

The importance of this for my argument regarding subjective realist multiform cinema is as follows. First, like the blockbuster, multiform cinema uses exhibitionistic forms. Further, like the blockbuster, it employs these forms in a primarily voyeuristic context (a realist narrative). The combination of exhibitionistic forms with a voyeuristic context in multiform cinema creates a tension similar to the kind that often leads to the dismissal of the blockbuster as unrealistic or fantastical. However, the difference between the two styles of filmmaking is that the exhibitinistic techniques employed in the multiform cinema (and complex narratives more generally) are not simply something amazing to behold, but are actually an integral part of the narrative structure of the film. Its effect on the audience may be similar—producing surprise, shock, or awe for instance—but its nature is radically different. It is based not in big-budget pyrotechnics or special effects, but in the manipulation of time, space, or narrative reality, as I will illustrate below. The techniques used are related to the tricks of Méliès, and these films combine experimental and/or unconventional narrative structures with fantastic elements to create stories that generate profound defamiliarization and uncanny experiences for spectators. These effects—often found in fantasy, horror, and science fiction films—are used in more realistic contexts, making their uncanniness all the more striking. Another way of putting this is that what these films offer is a kind of low-budget cinema of attractions, featuring complicated narrative structures that demand that spectators work much harder than they would to make meaning from the typical Hollywood film.

An extension of this is that there are several other similar types of attractions commonly employed in contemporary cinema. For example, performance can be seen as a type of attraction at the center of the star vehicle, a film designed primarily to show off the talents of a particular actor or actress.[6] (In the case of *Mulholland Drive*, Naomi Watts delivered a performance that launched her stardom.) Or, a better example comes from the work of Tanya Krzywinska, who writes: "in looking to hard-core [pornography] to win audience attention, European art cinema appears to be using the attraction of real sex to compete with the sensation-inducing spectacle of Hollywood's high-octane special effects laden blockbuster" (2005: 223). Examples of this trend include films such as *Romance* (Catherine Breillat 1999), *Intimacy* (Patrice Chereau 2001), *The Piano Teacher* (Michael Haneke 2001), and *9 Songs* (Michael Winterbottom 2004). In yet another view of the matter, Paul Ward explores the use of animation as "a specific type of spectacle," focusing on the uncanny impression *Waking Life*'s (Richard Linklater 2001) rotoscoping creates, calling it "spectacular realism" (2005: 163). These types of films can also be seen as examples of what I am calling the low-budget cinema of attractions, since they employ exhibitionistic elements—whether star performance, real sex, or rotoscoping—on comparatively modest budgets. The attractions offered by these films are similar to those developed in what Gunning describes as the avant-garde trajectory of the cinema of attractions, which we will consider now.

The Avant-Garde Trajectory: Realism and Defamiliarization

In Gunning's article, the avant-garde cinema of the twentieth century is seen to be directly influenced by the cinema of attractions. According to his account, many avant-garde filmmakers, initially excited by the possibilities of cinema yet disappointed in the realist path it followed, adapted particular elements of the cinema of attractions to their purposes. These artists were particularly inspired by the "trick films" of Méliès, which were the most common of the nonactuality form of the early cinema: plotless films made primarily for the purpose of demonstrating the "magical possibilities of the cinema" (Gunning 1990: 58). Trick films typically used manipulations like slow motion and multiple exposure to create their effects. An early example of the adaptation of these techniques for use in narrative cinema is the German silent film *The Student of Prague* (Paul Wegener 1913), in which Stellen Rye used stop-action cinematography to make characters disappear, as well as multiple exposure to allow them to reappear alongside their doppelgängers (Gunning 1990: 58). Films such as *The Student of Prague* were highly influential on the German Expressionist filmmakers of the following decades; German Expressionism was another movement notable for its exhibitionistic style. Luis Buñuel and Salvador Dalí used stop-action cinematography, discontinuity editing, and other techniques to radically disrupt the temporal, spatial, and causal dimensions of their surrealist classic *Un Chien Andalou* (Luis Buñuel 1929), which shocked and mystified its audiences. *Un Chien Andalou* was immensely influential on subsequent generations of filmmakers, and its influence can still be seen in films such as *Eternal Sunshine*, for instance.

The Student of Prague and *Un Chien Andalou* are typical of the ways in which the techniques of the trick film were employed by avant-garde artists. They also provide examples of the ways in which art cinema broke with classical conventions to disrupt narrative coherence, temporal continuity, and stable space. The disruptiveness of these characteristics is part of what might be seen as an important aesthetic trait of art cinema:

its rejection of the transparent, voyeuristic realism of the classical style. Bolter and Grusin use the term "hypermediacy" to describe different media that disrupt conventions in order to disrupt the type of transparent immediacy they normally create. "Hypermediacy," in this sense, is another way of describing an aesthetic style that calls attention to mediation rather than seeking to occlude it. Art cinema built on the exhibitionistic aspects of the cinema of attractions to intentionally disrupt immediacy. These disruptions are often in the service of an overt challenge to classical realism and as such are forms of hypermediation in Bolter and Grusin's use of the term. Interestingly, however, the challenge they issue to the classical realist style is not necessarily a rejection of "realism" per se; in fact, art cinema can be said to share certain goals with classical realism, even if the way it seeks to achieve these goals is quite different: "Hypermedia and transparent media are opposite manifestations of the same desire: to get past the limits of representation and to achieve the real" (2000: 53). The classical style seeks to transcend mediation through the erasure of the boundary between the real and the represented, whereas art cinema foregrounds the very same boundary. What is important to both, however, is the experience they evoke. In classical cinema, immediacy is the goal; for art cinema, the goal is authenticity. The authenticity it seeks results not from immersing spectators in transparent forms of representation, but from jolting them into an awareness of the mediated nature of cinema, and consequently (or at least, ideally) into an awareness of the experience of mediation itself.

In this sense, Bolter and Grusin's hypermediacy can be seen in its relationship to the Russian formalist Viktor Shklovsky's notion of "defamiliarization, the overall process whereby technique calls attention to the object" (Andrew 1976: 82–83). In the art cinema, continuity with the everyday world is not always what is important. In fact, it is often equally important to distort the world, as well as to disrupt the forms regularly employed to represent it. Art cinema is "formalist" in this sense. It seeks to make the familiar strange, alienating the spectator from the forms of representation they have become accustomed to—often defined in terms of classical realist cinema. In distorting the conventional, these forms make the experience of viewing more authentic, or more real. Shklovsky's notion of defamiliarization was widely circulated and highly influential on the literature and the visual arts of the day, and the relationship between his idea and the films of avant-garde artists is clear: these films used the aesthetics of attraction in the service of defamiliarization. The ends to which these techniques might be used vary, of course. For formalists like Shklovsky, they may be employed for no other reason than to increase the spectator's aesthetic enjoyment. For Brecht and Eisenstein, on the other hand, defamiliarization was employed for more practical, political purposes.

An unfortunate consequence of Shklovsky's influence was the rise of the idea that *only* defamiliarized material was worthwhile. This led to the view that conventional forms could not, by their very nature, be artistic, which, in turn, led many artists and theorists to reject conventional forms altogether in favor of totally defamiliarized forms. And, hierarchies of artistic merit were created based purely on a quantitative analysis of defamiliarization in a given text: e.g., 8½ is more artistic than *Vertigo* (Alfred Hitchcock 1958) because it contains ten more examples of defamiliarization. The logical conclusion to this sort of reasoning for cinema was that only experimental films of the most radical kind were artistic and that narrative cinema of any sort is, by its very nature, too conventional. Fortunately, in a second wave of formalism, which grew out a movement known as the Prague School, these extremes were tempered, and the notion of defamiliarization was refined.

The Prague School introduced the idea of *foregrounding* in its work on poetry, which drew attention to the fact that artistic speech is dependent on the conventional, codified speech of the everyday for its effect. Poetry stands out from the quotidian through its difference, and often through its difficulty, and, in this way, "lifts itself outside the readily understandable" (Andrew 1976: 82). Another way of thinking about this is simply to say that defamiliarization can only take place when there is a background of familiar forms from which the defamiliarized can be distinguished; it is most effective when it takes place in a naturalistic context. When it does not, it may become too difficult, abstract, or even meaningless.

William Earle, in an article entitled "Revolt Against Realism in the Films" (1968) divides cinema into four distinct theoretical categories,[7] and a consideration of how the films in each of these categories employ the techniques of defamiliarization offers an insight into the way some different views of defamiliarization are expressed cinematically. Earle's first category is *Realism*, which he describes along similar lines to those used above to describe classical narrative cinema: realist cinema is concerned with the transparent presentation of psychologically believable, clearly motivated characters moving through a coherent and recognizable time and space (Earle 1968: 37). In contrast to realist cinema, Earle's other categories are defined by their opposition to realism, and each employs, to some degree or other, the aesthetics of defamiliarization. The first is what he calls *Sensory Cinema*, which simply rejects all of the conventions of realism and removes "any possibility of perceiving real identities through them" (1968: 37). Sensory cinema, as Earle describes it, then, is built entirely on distortion and defamiliarization. There is no "foregrounding" since there is no (conventional) background. It is a purely abstract cinema, of the type made by Stan Brakhage, for instance. (See *Mothlight* [1963], *Black Ice* [1994], or *Water for Maya* [2000].)

Earle's next category, *Surrealism*, also represents a revolt against realism; however, it retains a somewhat less antagonistic relation to realism than Sensory Cinema, as its name suggests: "The surreal world, unlike that of sensory art, is indeed a world and is populated by identities; it is a world composed of things drawn from the real world but now de- or sur-realized; they are set free from their public or scientific connections and places in order to live a life of their own. Perhaps the most general name for such a feeling is dislocation; for if the very meanings of the things and persons we encounter derive from their relations to their proper places, a dislocation will show that object in a new light" (1968: 37). Surrealist cinema is more grounded in the everyday world than sensory cinema. Even though it dislocates the everyday from the conventional meanings and associations it accrues, it retains meaningful (recognizable) points of reference through which spectators may orient themselves. Surrealist cinema can be said to employ foregrounding, then, since however dislocated the world of the film may be, there is still enough of the conventional for the defamiliarized to stand out. *Un Chien Andalou* is a clear example of a surrealist film: it is not purely abstract, but it is purely oneiric. Its logic is not that of realism but of the dream.

Earle's final category, *Ironic Film*, "call[s] attention to the image, while still employing it as an image" (1968: 40). He writes, "Here our experience would be an ironic one, doubly aware of both the scene passing before our eyes and of our seeing it through images" (40). Ironic films use defamiliarized forms in a more or less realistic setting, and it is in this category that Earle situates the work of Fellini, Bergman, and Godard, for instance; it is also within this category that the subjective realist multiform cinema falls. There are two related ideas that are of particular interest regarding Ironic cinema, and both center on the idea of the calling of attention to the image, while still employing it as an image. First, in its reflexivity, Ironic cinema troubles the purely voyeuristic mode of realism, establishing a more complicated mode of viewing. It does this by disrupting the transparent immediacy of realism, while still employing it to some degree. A second, and closely related, point is that Ironic cinema, unlike sensory (experimental) cinema, maintains a representational background upon which defamiliarization takes place. It should be noted that more often than not, Ironic cinema employs the conventions of the classical style to create this background. It does not seek to create a totally or mostly defamiliarized frame of reference; it does, however, foreground artifice rather than hiding it, usually in a largely naturalistic context. The double awareness experienced by the spectator results from his or her being absorbed in a narrative, and yet aware of the formal and constructed nature of the narrative. Ironic cinema as it described by Earle remains close to the realism it revolts against, but not so close as to be mistaken for it. In this sense, much of what has been considered art cinema is ironic. Earle's notion of the revolt against realism provides an interesting framework for considering the ways in which defamiliarization has been employed in the cinema, and in the broader terms of my argument, each of Earle's latter three categories employs what I have referred to as the aesthetics of attraction, and each sits on what Gunning refers to as the avant-garde trajectory of the cinema of attractions. It is, however, this last category that is of particular interest, since subjective realist multiform films are clearly a type of Ironic cinema.

The subjective realist multiform narratives used in *Mulholland Drive*, *Memento*, and *Eternal Sunshine* are exhibitionistic forms that disrupt the cinematic conventions aimed at creating an absorptive mode of viewing. Multiform films from *Caligari* to *The Fountain* are intensely aware of their relationship to spectators and their expectations, and although they often employ the narrative and aesthetic conventions of the classical style, they invariably challenge, disrupt, and distort this style as well. As such, subjective realist multiform cinema can be understood in terms of the way in which it works both with and against conventionality to produce its effects. Chapter 3 will explore some of the many aesthetic and narrative techniques employed in multiform cinema, particularly those used to present the subjective perspective of a character to create a style described by David Bordwell as *subjective realism*.

Notes

1. This voyeuristic dimension of narrative cinema has, of course, been widely discussed in film studies, particularly by psychoanalytic theorists in the 1970s and 80s, and most notably by Laura Mulvey in "Visual Pleasure and Narrative Cinema" (1989).
2. Bolter and Grusin's version of immediacy is not rooted in this type of foundationalist epistemology, but rather has parallels to poststructuralist theory, particularly to Derrida's notion of mimesis, in which mimesis is defined not in terms of a correlation between a representation and the object it represents (sign to signified or image to reality), but in terms of the resemblance between one representation and another (sign to sign or image to image).
3. Douglas Trumball's *Brainstorm* (1983) features a similar device.
4. It is this aspect of the classical narrative style that is often critiqued. For example, Marxists see it as hiding the bourgeois ideological elements and psychoanalytic critics see it as masking the role cinema plays in generating fantasy worlds for its viewers. Others simply note the impossibility of this type of immersion.

5. There are of course other contexts in which the critique of spectacle arises. For my purposes here and now, however, I am focused primarily on the way these bear on narrative.
6. In the mid 1990s, many stars began appearing in low-budget independent features as a way of broadening their star images. The success of this ploy has turned the practice into the rule rather than the exception, occasionally blurring the boundary between the star-vehicle and the independent feature (as well as sending budgets for these films higher and higher).
7. That the categories are "theoretical" is important, since no perfectly pure example of these forms as he describes them is likely to exist.

Chapter 3

SUBJECTIVE REALISM AND MULTIFORM NARRATIVES

The classical Hollywood style, as we have seen, achieves its verisimilitude, in part, by seeking to hide the gap that separates it from reality. It aims to create believable characters located in a coherent space-time setting using naturalistic mise-en-scène and continuity editing. This style is dominant the world over and is the default mode of realist narration for visual storytellers. There are, however, other styles and definitions of realism, many of which have arisen in opposition to the classical style. This oppositional tendency was briefly considered in chapter 1 in relation to the way unconventional narrative styles have been seen to more adequately reflect the experiences of the characters depicted. When considering the contexts from which the subjective realist multiform cinema has emerged, this argument seems to have some traction. *The Cabinet of Dr. Caligari* (Robert Weine 1919), which can be seen as one of the first instances of a subjective realist multiform film, was made in a devastated post–World War I Germany; and later instances, such as 8½ and *Rashomon*, arose in similar contexts. The differences between these films and their Hollywood counterparts were undoubtedly the result of a conscious effort on the part of filmmakers to create an authentic representation of their experience of life after two immensely destructive wars, whether in the Weimar Republic or the post–World War II period in Italy, France, Japan, or Sweden. As a stylistic alternative to classical realism, then, the subjective realist style used in these films could be said to have been developed as an attempt to more accurately depict the existential crisis of the postwar era.

Multiform cinema, as I have defined it, is built on the subjective realist style of narration, which depicts the imagination of a character from a subjective point of view. This subjective perspective is what Bruce Kawin refers to as a "mindscreen": the presentation of what a character *thinks*, rather than a more objective depiction of what he or she does (Kawin 1978: 10). David Bordwell, in his work on art cinema narration, describes "subjective realism" as a style of filmmaking that "deals with the reality of the imagination . . . as if it were as real as the world before us" (1985: 206). Subjective realist multiform narratives employ this type of narration in at least one of the strands of a dual- or multi-stranded narrative. The subjective realist strand represents the experience of a character in the film as if it were as real as other levels of narration. What I want to do now is consider some of the formal characteristics of subjective realism in more detail, as well as considering a number films that serve as precursors to the contemporary examples I will consider in later chapters.

Subjective Realism

Ruth Perlmutter, in discussing the relationship of films such as *Last Year at Marienbad* (Alain Resnais 1961), *Mulholland Drive,* and *Memento* to the quintessential "trance film," *Meshes of the Afternoon* (Maya Deren 1943), lists some of the important stylistic traits of subjective realism. In addition to articulating many of the characteristics that bind these films together stylistically, Perlmutter also identifies many of the characteristics of what I am calling multiform narratives. She writes that the trance film—a term that has been used primarily in reference to the experimental cinema of Deren—features:

> 1. Voyages into interior states of mind; 2. Various stages of sleep, dream, daydreams and awakenings which blur the distinctions between dream and reality; 3. What-if narratives that entertain more than one scenario in order to alter an unacceptable outcome; 4. Complex (often paralyzing) plots that reject single-line character logic and incorporate other modes. 5. The use of psychosomatic symptoms and destructive impulses as an evasion of uncomfortable reality; 6. A flight from the self as a metaphor for escape from entrapment by cinema; 7. A pervasive atmosphere of crisis that causes a breakdown in the film text, taxing the viewer's memory, comprehension and interpretation. (Perlmutter 2005: 133–34)

Numbers one and two of this list refer to (subjective realist) narration; three and four describe the effects of this style of narration on the way information is presented and, thus, the effects on the narrative itself; and five through seven explain how and why the above strategies are used: e.g., the central characters of the films suffer various psychological disorders and hide "behind [these] psychic maladies in an effort to seek a new identity or escape into alternative selves" (Perlmutter 2005: 125). Perlmutter's article identifies many of the formal techniques used to represent the psychic conditions of these characters including surrealist visual motifs, embedded narratives, fragmented temporalities, unsynched sound and image juxtapositions, and oneiric causal logic (Perlmutter 2005: 126). These aesthetic and narrative characteristics are designed to produce in spectators an experience similar to that of the trance film's dreaming, psychotic, or maladjusted characters. The ways in which these characters' disintegrating subjectivities are represented strain the conventions of realism. Perlmutter offers an example from Bergman's *Persona* in which there is a visual distortion that results from what appears to be the film burning on the lamp of the projector, "as if [the film is] responding with its own trauma to Alma's adoption of [Elizabeth's] destructive behavior" (2005: 126). In *Mulholland Drive*, which overtly references *Persona* on several occasions, there is a similar distortion that takes place as Betty and Rita flee the apartment of Diane Selwyn after discovering a decaying corpse. In this scene, the film seems to slip from the cogs of the projector, making the sprocket perforations of the actual filmstrip visible. This apparent malfunction briefly disrupts the illusion created by the act of projection and can be seen to reflect the trauma experienced by the characters in their encounter with death. It also provides a clue that this episode takes place in the context of a dream that itself is structured like a film.

Perlmutter's work maps much of the terrain on which the subjective realist multiform cinema sits and her analysis of trance films indirectly offers a glimpse at the way in which subjective realist narration is used not simply to represent the imagination of an unstable character, but also to produce a feeling of instability in the spectator struggling to make sense of the film. It is both interesting and useful in relationship to multiform narrative and subjective realist narration, for it clearly demonstrates the similarities between contemporary complex narrative cinema and the more experimental works of Maya Deren. So, although the context of Perlmutter's work is an analysis of trance films, the characteristics she describes are clearly related to, and often synonymous with, those of the subjective realist multiform film. The key difference between the trance film and the subjective realist multiform film is that the former—*Meshes of the Afternoon* is a case in point—emerged from very different production contexts and is classified as experimental rather than narrative or feature film. What Perlmutter demonstrates through her article, however, is the indebtedness of contemporary films such as *Mulholland Drive* and *Memento* to the work of filmmakers such as Deren. With this in mind, I want to consider how multiform cinema, built on the subjective realist style, might be argued to provide a more truthful or authentic representation of experience than the classical style.

Janet Murray, in *Hamlet on the Holodeck* (1997), does indeed propose that complex narratives may actually provide a more accurate representation of the world we live in and of the type of subjectivity we experience. She argues that the scientific and technological innovations of our age have brought about an experience of reality that requires different narrative forms to adequately render, proposing multiform narrative as one of a number of different styles that offer something unified linear narrative styles cannot. Slavoj Žižek, in his analysis of David Lynch's *Lost Highway*, echoes Murray's point where he writes: "a new 'life experience' is in the air, a perception of life that explodes the form of the linear centered narrative and renders life as a multiform flow" (2000: 39). Like Murray, Žižek suggests that multiform narratives offer a way of representing reality that may be more truthful, or truth-like, than unified narratives. In this view, subjective realist multiform films can be seen as an alternative to classical realism, one that opposes it in an effort to forge a more authentic representation of certain types of experience.

Subjective realist multiform cinema, of course, is not new, nor is the subjective realism it employs any less constructed or conventional than any other style of realism. Unlike the "wire" in *Strange Days* (Kathryn Bigelow 1995) it cannot literally place spectators in the mind of a character either. What subjective realist multiform cinema does offer, however, is a type of realism that approximates for the spectator something resembling the direct experience of a character in the film. These characters are often traumatized, and their experience of the world is far from average. *Memento*, for example, offers spectators an experience of what it might be like to have anterograde amnesia, and it does so through a style of narration that radically complicates the cause-effect relationships between events. Similarly, *Eternal Sunshine* seeks to represent what it might be like to have one's memory erased while still, in some sense, conscious (and it draws on numerous visual tropes of experimental cinema to do so). Finally, the narrative complexity of *Mulholland Drive* directly parallels its psychotic central character's own struggle to narrate her experience, while the spectator's difficulty making sense of the fragmented plot directly parallels Diane's struggle. Although these films are not realist in a classical sense, they can be argued to be *realistic* in a subjective sense, since they are attempting to represent the experience of their psychically disturbed central characters.

While the trance film and other examples from experimental cinema offer useful points of reference for considering subjective realist narration, there are other sources, as we have seen. What I would like to do now is consider the way in which subjective realism has been employed in Hollywood. To do this, I will begin with an analysis of two examples from *Vertigo*, considering the aesthetic techniques used in these scenes and the type of response they are designed to evoke.

Vertigo

I begin with *Vertigo* because it is typical of the manner in which Hollywood cinema has traditionally employed subjective realist narration. The scenes I will consider represent Scottie's dreams and altered states of consciousness, and the first example takes place in the opening sequence of the film, where the *reverse-tracking forward-zoom shot*, (or "zolly") is used, not simply just to visually represent Scottie's experience of vertigo, but to actually create an approximation for spectators of what it might actually feel like to experience acrophobia-induced vertigo. The technique was actually created for the film. The second example of subjective realist narration occurs later in *Vertigo* when a dream sequence is rendered through the blending of live-action footage and animation to create a series of oneiric special effects. The dream—like Scottie's experience of vertigo—is represented in a way that breaks with the continuity style and presents spectators with a first-person account of the events taking place in the dream. In this sequence, however, the disruption of continuity is greater than the disruption in the representation of vertigo since it distorts not simply the visual space, but also the temporality and causal relationships that have characterized the film up to this point. As such, it is another example of the exhibitionistic aesthetics employed in *Vertigo* to represent the subjective realist perspective of its central character.

Vertigo offers two separate forms of realism in the same narrative space. It shifts from an objective, observational realism, represented via the continuity style, to a first-person, subjective realism represented through a hypermediated style. The use of the two side by side in *Vertigo* is typical of Hollywood cinema in which subjective realism is used to represent dreams, hallucinations, altered states of consciousness, and mental disorders. The important thing about the examples from *Vertigo*, and what makes them typical of the continuity style, is that these subjective realist moments are clearly marked as deviations from the norm: *this is Scottie's experience of vertigo*; and *this is a dream*. When clearly marked like this, shifts from one ontology to another are easily comprehensible for spectators as continuity is maintained. The same cannot be said of those that are not marked.

In many multiform films, subjective realist narration is used to represent alternate realities constituting entire narrative strands. The shifts into or out of these strands are not always accompanied by clear markers but are woven into the broader narrative fabric of the film without any clear indication of their ontological status. *Mulholland Drive*, for example, features a dream sequence that comprises well over half the film, and, although it can be argued that the sequence is marked as a dream, it is by no means *clearly* marked (as the critical writing on the film makes evident). As a result, multiform films such as *Mulholland Drive* make greater demands on spectators than films that wholly employ the continuity style. The techniques these films use can be thought of as different types of defamiliarization. Just as poetry often distorts conventional language to produce its effects, so, the subjective realist multiform film defamiliarizes the commonplace representations of the world offered by conventional cinema.

Torben Grodal has attempted to create an inventory of the types of distortions used in cinema to evoke "larger than life" responses in spectators. He calls these "subjectivity elicitors," though they might also simply be considered techniques used to create defamiliarized forms of representation. I want to briefly consider the particular forms described by Grodal that are common to subjective realist narration and multiform cinema. Grodal, like Bordwell, uses a theoretical framework derived from cognitive psychology to develop his ideas, and he describes the feelings evoked by these techniques as resulting from, among other things, the inability of a spectator to make meaning from the information he or she encounters. Many of the techniques described by Grodal are not directly relevant to the films under discussion here, and in the interest of space, I will limit my summary to those that are.[1] The first of these occurs when "perceptual access to a represented space is deviating or distorted" (Grodal 2000: 93). There are a broad range of techniques of this type in the cinema, and one such distortion is based on the use of nonanthropomorphic shot scale, where the use of extreme long shots situate both characters and spectators in a passive relationship to the objects and space represented. Extreme long shots—of mountains, or the earth from outer space, for example—create different types of associations than those created by close-ups or medium shots and can be used to make human action seem insignificant, alienating spectators from the action. It is quite possible to imagine picking up a coffee cup that is shot in close-up, but what is to be done with an extreme long shot of the World Trade Center as it is blown to dust and rubble? The feeling of passivity created may evoke emotional experiences of helplessness or awe. Other visual distortions based in cinematography, including ultra-close-ups or unusual framing, shot-scale, or angles all have the potential to "make recognition difficult and provide feelings of unfamiliarity" (Grodal 2000: 95). Many of these techniques are used in subjective realist narration, often to represent the perceptual limitations of a character. Indeed, these techniques can also be used in conjunction with other strategies to position spectators in close relationship with a character whose own restricted perspective results in inaccurate or problematic interpretations of the diegetic world of the film. *Mulholland Drive*, *Memento*, and *Eternal Sunshine*, for example, all limit narrative information almost solely to what their central characters know, or what they think they know, and then exploit the limitations of this perspective for dramatic purposes.

Grodal's list includes another related set of techniques that he describes as seeking "to simulate mental process" (2000: 98). He cites the cinematic representation of memory, dreams, and hallucinations as examples of techniques that deviate from normal representations; in other words, subjective realism. Subjective realist narration, when used to represent memory and imagination, follows a logic different from that of continuity-style narration. Spatial and temporal disruptions in the subjective realist worlds of multiform films are to be expected since the cognitive frameworks used to navigate dreams, imagination, and memory are different from those that order our waking life. Further, as the representations of dreams, memories, hallucinations, and other states of consciousness are the central building blocks of multiform cinema, narrative fragmentation—whether temporal, spatial, causal, or ontological—is a logical characteristic. *Mulholland Drive*, *Memento*, and *Eternal Sunshine*, as well as earlier instances of multiform cinema like *Caligari*, *Wild Strawberries*, and *8½*, all feature disruptions of these kinds.

The last of Grodal's categories I want to consider concerns what he describes as "situations with a problematic reality status" (Grodal 2000: 99). He writes about the ways in which unexplainable or seemingly supernatural events can evoke complicated responses in viewers. Unexplainable events are common in multiform cinema for the same reason narrative fragmentation is: what is represented is taking place inside a character's mind. In films that employ subjective realist narration to represent the experience of a character—particularly their dreams, memories, or hallucinations—unexplainable events often play a central role. The unexplainable events of multiform narratives are often the result of unmarked ontological shifts and subjective realism, and the effects these produce on audiences can be better understood using a framework developed by theorist Tzvetan Todorov. The categories Todorov provides for classifying such events are useful in specifying the differences and similarities in multiform films from 8½ to *Eternal Sunshine* (1973: 25).

The Fantastic

As we have seen in the consideration of early cinema, magical events have been important to filmmaking since the days of Méliès, who developed the trick film as a means of exploiting the potential of the cinema to amaze spectators. In later years, unexplainable and/or magical events were occasionally woven into narrative films, and ultimately, entire movements and genres were built around the marriage of special effects and narrative. Tzvetan Todorov's work on "the fantastic," although primarily concerned with literature, is useful for analyzing films in which cinematic manipulations are used to present spectators with unexplainable events in the course of a narrative. "The fantastic" provides both a framework for understanding how these tricks operate on the spectator as well as categories for articulating differences between a number of different types of such events. The fantastic comprises what Todorov calls a "theoretical genre"; however, it can also be understood as an exhibitionistic narrative technique for producing the type of defamiliarization described by Shkvlosky (1973: 25).

The key features of a "fantastic" narrative are a naturalistic setting and an event that cannot be readily explained naturalistically. According to Todorov, "the fantastic is that hesitation experienced by a person who knows only the laws of nature confronting an apparently supernatural event" (1973: 25). The spectator of *Mulholland Drive*, for instance, is faced with just such an event when the character Betty simply disappears near the end of the film's first movement. Her disappearance does not fit the relatively naturalistic context of the narrative to this point. Spectators are left with a set of unanswerable questions at the end of the film's first movement: Where has Betty gone? How? And, why? The fantastic arises when an unexplainable event such as this takes place in a narrative in which events of this type are not expected, that is, when set in a similar world to that of the spectators (as opposed to those of fantasy, horror, or science fiction for instance). Todorov argues that the experience he describes can *only* occur in fiction set "in a world which is indeed our world, the one we know—a world without devils, sylphides, or vampires" (1973: 25). The reason for this is simple: in fantasy and science fiction narratives, when animals speak or time and space warp, the spectator does not struggle to understand these events but rather accepts them as conventions of the genre. The fantastic, by contrast, arises when a seemingly supernatural event disrupts a *naturalistic* diegetic world. So, when Betty Elms mysteriously vanishes from her aunt's bedroom in *Mulholland Drive*, the disappearance disrupts the expectations of its spectators since it is unexplainable in the naturalistic context of the first movement of the film.

Another such example occurs in *Being John Malkovich*, when Craig Schwartz (John Cusack) discovers—behind a filing cabinet in his office—a portal that allows him first-person access to the mind of actor John Malkovich. In this instance, the portal, which is unexplainable by the natural laws known by the spectator, arises in a naturalistic context, and so, ushers the spectator into the ambiguous zone of the fantastic. Todorov writes of the kind of experience this evokes: "The person who experiences the event must opt for one of two possible solutions: either he is the victim of an illusion of the senses, of a product of the imagination—and laws of the world then remain what they are; or else the event has indeed taken place, it is an integral part of reality—but then this reality is controlled by laws unknown to us. . . . The fantastic occupies the duration of this uncertainty" (Todorov 1973: 25). The fantastic, then, is the state of indecision on the part of the spectator created by the unexplainable event. It is the cognitive hesitation that results from the lack of sufficient information required to make a decision regarding the nature of the event. In narrative terms, the fantastic can be understood as a disruption of causality. These events raise, often very forcefully, questions such as: How can this event be explained in the context of this narrative? What caused it and does it make sense? If it does not make sense, the spectator is placed in a position where the unexplainable causal dimension of the narrative must be accounted for and yet cannot be—at least not on the basis of information provided by the narrative thus far. The cognitive hesitation on the spectator's part is the necessary first condition of the fantastic. Very often, however, the hesitation experienced by the spectator is also shared by characters in the narrative as well. In *Mulholland Drive*, for instance, Betty's disappearance is mysterious not only to the spectator but also to Rita, whose response to the event is chilling.

Another example of shared hesitation can be found in *Fight Club*, where the spectator and the film's central character, "Jack" (Edward Norton), experience the same response to the revelation that Tyler Durden (Brad Pitt) is actually Jack's alter ego—a doppelgänger rather than an actual person. *Fight Club* achieves its twist by restricting the narration so that the spectator shares the limited (and pathological) perspective of the narrator Jack, who is suffering from a dissociative identity disorder. The "fantastic" moment in the film is built around a narration that, for over an hour, has included regular interactions between Jack and Tyler, played by two different actors. This has led spectators to the conclusion that they are two distinct human beings; and yet, they are not. The hesitation that follows the revelation is shared by both the protagonist and the spectator.[2] Jack is as shocked by the revelation as the spectator is and both are without the means of explaining how it can be possible. This type of shared experience, though not requisite to the Todorovian notion of the fantastic, is common. The fantastic, by definition, places the spectator in a relationship with the unexplainable event, which makes an informed decision regarding its nature impossible. The event that initiates the fantastic may ultimately be explained, or it may not be, but until an explanation is provided, or until a decision is made by the spectator regardless of the provision of an explanation, the spectator remains in the mode of the fantastic.

For the spectator of *Being John Malkovich*, this state is maintained from the time of Craig's initial entry into Malkovich's head to the point at which an explanation (supernatural) for the event is offered (to both Craig and the spectator) later in the film. In *Fight Club*, the explanation is provided almost immediately through a series of rapid shots that replay earlier scenes. These shots offer an economical visual explanation of the stunning revelation, dispensing with any further doubt on the part of the spectator. (*Mulholland Drive* is seen by some critics as withholding an explanation, which means that responsibility for the resolution of the conundrum is left in the hands of spectators who must decide for themselves how to make sense of the events.) Once an explanation is provided or a decision is made regarding the unexplainable event, the "hesitation" ends and a neighboring "genre" is entered (Todorov 1973: 25). Todorov writes, "the fantastic leads a life full of dangers, and may evaporate at any moment. It seems located on the frontier of two genres rather than to be an autonomous genre" (Todorov 1973: 41). Todorov's argument is that once the event is explained, there is a shift out of the mode of the fantastic, into one of two possible "genres" neighboring the fantastic, the *uncanny* and the *marvelous*; or into one of two intermediary "subgenres," the *fantastic uncanny* and the *fantastic marvelous*.

These four categories are important to Todorov's model since the concept of the fantastic is extremely narrow and always temporary, and, since fantastic narratives will invariably resolve into one of these four other types. Even if *Mulholland Drive* offers no explanation, for instance, the spectator must decide how to explain the event. Betty's disappearance may be supernatural, for instance, or it may be the result of a trick, or some other explanation may be decided upon. If narrative meaning is to be made, some explanation must be conjectured. In films like *Mulholland Drive*, the fantastic is explainable on the basis of the subjective realist nature of the narration. My reading of *Mulholland Drive*, for instance, is that the events that conclude the first movement of the film are explainable by their oneiric origins: the unexplainable makes sense when understood in the context of a dream. The result of this explanation is a shift out of the fantastic and into the first of Todorov's neighboring categories, the uncanny. (An alternate explanation is that the events are supernatural, making the shift in the direction of the marvelous.) The uncanny occurs when, in the course of the narrative, an explanation is provided that causes the spectator to decide that "the laws of reality remain intact and permit an explanation of the phenomena described" (Todorov 1973: 41): "events are related which may be readily accounted for by the laws of reason, but which are, in one way or another, incredible, extraordinary, shocking, singular, disturbing or unexpected, and thereby provoke in the character and reader a reaction similar to that which works of the fantastic have made familiar" (Todorov 1973: 46). The uncanny is a wide category then and the one I believe *Fight Club* most readily fits into as well, since the events it recounts are quite extraordinary, even though they are readily explainable. Similarly, the shock of *Memento*, as we shall see, is derived more from the manner in which it recounts the events, rather than the nature of the events themselves. That is to say, Leonard's condition, which the narration simulates, is uncanny rather than unexplainable or supernatural.

The marvelous, which sits on the opposite end of the continuum from the uncanny, results when "new laws of nature must be entertained to account for the phenomena" (Todorov 1973: 41). Examples of marvelous narratives, as Todorov describes them, are numerous, and one need only look to the fantasy genre to find them. Films such as *The Lord of the Rings* (Peter Jackson 2001) are marvelous in that their "supernatural elements provoke no particular reaction in either the characters or in the implicit reader" (Todorov 1973: 52). This is because they are set in worlds where the rules and physical laws of our own familiar world do not apply. Science fiction cinema might also be seen as marvelous, as it often features futuristic technologies that are foreign and even impossible given our present state of knowledge.

Todorov's intermediate genre of the fantastic marvelous, however, is slightly different and is described as "the class of narratives that are presented as fantastic and that end with an acceptance of the supernatural" (1973: 52). This is possible because fantastic-marvelous narratives are not set in another world, but in one familiar enough to spectators that a seemingly supernatural event will evoke a hesitation. So, as *Being*

John Malkovich has a naturalistic setting in which an unexplainable event occurs, and since it finally offers new laws of nature for the causal explanation of its characters' ability to enter the mind of John Malkovich, the film is "fantastic-marvelous." Its explanation of the seemingly unexplainable event is finally supernatural. However, its unexplainable events take place in a naturalistic setting rather than in one in which they are naturalized, as is the case with science fiction or fantasy.[3] (Another way of thinking about this category is through the lens of magic realism, a category that is as yet underdeveloped in film studies but bears further consideration.)

Finally, Todorov's fantastic uncanny describes "events that seemed supernatural throughout a story receive a rational explanation at its end" (Todorov 1973: 44). The supernatural is eroded in these types of stories through explanations including coincidences, dreams, the influence of drugs, tricks,[4] illusions of the senses, or madness (Todorov 1973: 45). This type of explanation is commonly found in multiform cinema. Although the fantastic events of *Mulholland Drive*, for example, have been explained by critics in a number of different ways, the vast majority sees the events as resulting from their oneiric origins, thus offering a fantastic-uncanny reading, as we shall see shortly.[5] Similarly, *Eternal Sunshine* can be described as fantastic-uncanny since its fantastic elements have a rational explanation: they are offering the subjective realist perspective of the film's central character as his memory is being systematically erased. The "fantastic" as described by Todorov, and as it is used in contemporary cinema, is another of the many aesthetic techniques employed in the low-budget cinema of attractions to generate its effects. The fantastic is relevant to the discussion of subjective realist narration because in the films under consideration, the two often go hand in hand. Subjective realist multiform films often feature fantastic moments which are themselves the result of a subjective realist narration. Now, I would like to conclude this chapter with a consideration of Ingmar Bergman's *Wild Strawberries* as an example of an subjective realist multiform film. I will focus on how some of the aesthetic and narrative forms described above are used in the film.

Wild Strawberries

Ingmar Bergman's *Wild Strawberries* is a quintessential example of subjective realist multiform cinema. Made in 1957, it makes extensive use of subjective realist narration to tell the story of Isak Borg, a medical doctor at the end of his career and nearing the end of his life. The story is based around the journey he takes to his hometown of Malmö, where his university is presenting him with an honorary degree. Isak is accompanied on the journey by his pregnant daughter-in-law Marianne, who is returning to her husband (Borg's son) after a month-long separation. Along the way, Isak and Marianne pick up a young woman named Sara and her two suitors, Viktor and Anders—the three of whom are hitchhiking around Sweden. The car journey structures the largely episodic narrative and serves as the backdrop for a series of conversations between Isak and the others on personal, philosophical, and theological matters, which in turn provide fodder for a series of dreams and flashback sequences in which Borg reflects on his childhood, his failures in life (including his disastrous marriage), and his mortality. The film features two levels of narration: the first is an objective level that tells the present-day story of Borg and his family; and the second, a series of subjective realist sequences, many of which represent Borg's past. These subjective sequences are made up of dreams and flashbacks, most of them traumatic.

Early in the film—its second scene, in fact—Isak recounts a dream (shown as an embedded narrative) that he has the night before he departs for Malmö. In it, he gets lost during his morning walk and finds himself wandering among abandoned houses and businesses in an unknown part of town. The streets are empty and unfamiliar, leaving Isak confused and unable to get his bearings. As fear begins to set in, the sound of his heartbeat accompanies an image of him sheltering in the shadow of a large clock mounted on the wall of the building where he stands. He looks at the clock and sees that it has no hands. He then looks at his own watch and discovers that it also lacks hands. He then turns and sees the figure of a man standing nearby, who has appeared as if from nowhere, and Isak approaches him for assistance. The man's back is turned and when Isak turns him around by the shoulder, the man's face is shown in close-up. It is bloated and horrific. The frightened Isak releases him, and the man falls to the ground where blood begins pouring from his head. Isak walks away in shock and immediately, a horse-drawn hearse laden with a coffin approaches. It has no driver and its rear wheel becomes stuck on a lamppost near Isak. The horse pulls the carriage until the rear wheel dislodges and nearly knocks Isak over. At the same time, the coffin tumbles off the hearse and onto the sidewalk in front of him, where the lid of the coffin is dislodged and the arm of its occupant protrudes. Borg, fearful but curious, walks closer to inspect the corpse, and as he draws near, he discovers that it is he himself in the coffin. At the moment this registers, Isak's doppelgänger seizes him by the hand and draws him near. The final shots of the sequence are a series of close-up shot/reverse-shots from the perspective of both Borg and his doppelgänger as their faces come closer together as

Isak is drawn toward the coffin. The effect is horrifying, and results in Isak awakening from his nightmare.

This sequence is notable for several reasons. First, it is one of two important dream sequences in the film and the first of its many subjective realist sequences. As such, the narrational shift to the dream is also the first of several ontological shifts that take place in *Wild Strawberries*. In this instance, it represents the move from the primary level of narration to an oneiric level and is clearly marked by a voice-over in which Isak states that he is recounting a dream. Next, the unconventional style of narration employed in the dream sequence clearly establishes a frame of reference for later similar sequences, each of which offers viewers a subjective account of Borg's memories. The temporal, spatial, and causal disruptions in this initial dream sequence are uncanny and establish a tone that continues in later scenes.

The second subjective realist sequence in *Wild Strawberries* occurs when Isak takes Marianne for a visit to his family's summer house. As he sits in the garden while Marianne has a swim, he remembers a series of events that took place when he was a young man. His memories are shown, once again, as an embedded narrative, and begin with his recollection of his brother Sigfried stealing a kiss from Isak's then fiancé, Sara. From this subjective realist sequence, the spectator learns that Sigfried ultimately convinces Sara to abandon Isak and marry him. Stylistically, although the sequence resembles a flashback, it is not. This is because Isak himself was not present for the events these scenes recount, so could not simply be remembering them. More importantly, during this sequence, Borg—the old man—has a conversation with his former fiancé—the young Sara—who explains to him why she chose Sigfried rather than him. This vignette provides another clear indication that the sequence is imaginative rather than simply a memory. Like Isak's dream, this flashback-like scene has a different ontological status with regard to the primary strand of the film. If the events portrayed are factually accurate—and there is no reason to suspect they are not—they can be viewed as reconstructions of events as they are imagined by Isak, now an old man sitting in the overgrown garden remembering back to one of his life's great humiliations. Like the dream represented earlier in the film, this sequence gives spectators a firsthand account of the subjective perspective of Isak, and, an approximate experience of the events he recalls. In this way, *Wild Strawberries* is a clear precursor to the type of subjective realist films that will be considered below.

Of the many films under consideration here, *Eternal Sunshine* is the one most similar to *Wild Strawberries* in that its departures from reality are similarly rooted in the memories of its central character. Although the departures are initially unmarked in *Eternal Sunshine*, the observant spectator quickly understands their nature. Similarly, the narratives of both *Wild Strawberries* and *Eternal Sunshine*, though complex, are generally coherent and employ the classical style in all but their subjective realist sequences. The spatial and causal disruptions of both films take place in these alternate ontological strands, offering spectators a type of first-person narration of memories refracted through imagination. *Wild Strawberries* is one of many films from the art cinema of the twentieth century that employs a subjective realist style of narration to tell its story. Although it is not as opaque as Bergman's later contribution, *Persona*, it is an important point of reference for contemporary examples, one of which I would like to consider now.

Notes

1. The first of Grodal's subjective elicitors occurs in film sequences with "little or no action and little or no cause for focused propositions" (Grodal 2000: 93). Scenes in which little or nothing happens cause spectators to "search for meaning by activating unfocussed associations" (2000: 93). Grodal suggests that the films of Andrei Tarkovsky feature numerous examples of these type of scenes and "rely on a more select audience that are strongly motivated for a subjective, lyrical search" (2000: 93). The second type of elicitor results when "a represented space impedes perceptual access" and Grodal focuses on visual impediments like "fog, rain, darkness, complex assemblies of objects with blurred and unsharp mutual delimitation" as potential visual sources used to create an impeded perceptual frame; if spectators cannot clearly see what is happening, their imaginations will be forced to take over (2000: 93-94). Examples of this type of elicitor include the wet, foggy streets of film noir, and Grodal cites the continuous rain in the early scenes of David Fincher's *Se7en* as an example of how it is used to create "a claustrophobic feeling of lack of control" (2000: 94). I would add to this an example of how auditory impediments might create similar effects: in one version of David Lynch's *Fire Walk With Me* (1992) there is an extended scene that takes place in a nightclub and features a seemingly important conversation, which is nonetheless completely inaudible to spectators due to loud music. Another elicitor "relates to representations of deviant emotional phenomena and reactions" and Grodal describes how a "subjectivizing effect is created by blocking normal empathic feelings" (2000: 100). This technique is interesting to consider in relation to many of the smart films and their lack of affect (Sconce 2002: 93).
2. George Wilson, in an article on what he calls "twist movies," discusses the way in which restricted narration can be used to generate epistemic shifts for audiences. The twist movie derives its power from the presentation of subjective frameworks in an unmarked manner so that that knowledgeability is limited to the central character's subjective experience. To restate this in terms of my own argument, the twist movie uses unmarked ontological shifts and subjective realist narration to create its effect. The unique element of the films Wilson is interested in is derived through presenting spectators with a limited perspective on the action of the story and then revealing these limits, which usually occur concurrently with the character's own epiphan-

ic moment. In *Fight Club*, for instance, the epistemological epiphany occurs when spectators realize, along with Jack, that Tyler Durden is actually Jack's alter ego. In *Memento*, the twist happens when Teddy informs Leonard (and the audience) that his wife survived the attack, and died later of an overdose of insulin administered by Leonard himself (although the reliability of Teddy's account remains ambiguous). *Mulholland Drive* could also be argued to be a twist film, and is indeed mentioned by Wilson. The "twist" of the twist movie can be thought of in terms of Todorov's fantastic. The unexplainable or shocking elements of the plot are explained by the revelation of subjective realist nature of the narration.

3. Of course, it is possible to read *Malkovich* as an allegory, in which case it could be said to be a "marvelous" narrative.
4. M. Night Shyamalan's *The Village* (2004) is an example of a type of trick film in this sense. *The Village*, which followed Shyamalan's wildly successful supernatural thriller *The Sixth Sense*, plays on its spectator's expectations of a supernatural story but subverts these in a twist that reveals the monsters of the film to be village elders masquerading in an attempt to keep its younger members in fear of the outside world. In other words, the film offers a naturalistic explanation for the seemingly supernatural events. Another fantastic-uncanny film in which the unexplainable events prove to be the result of a trick is Christopher Nolan's *The Prestige* (2006). Robert Angier (Hugh Jackman) is obsessed with his rival Alfred Borden's (Christian Bale) latest magic trick and becomes convinced that it is indeed based in the supernatural. The disappearing act, however, is ultimately revealed to be a trick of perception made possible by the fact that Borden has an identical twin brother. The seemingly supernatural event is, after all, an illusion. (In yet another twist, however, Angier is enabled to reproduce Borden's feat through supernatural means!)
5. A small group of others explain the film on supernatural grounds.

Chapter 4

MULHOLLAND DRIVE

Mulholland Drive, like each of the films I will consider, features multiple narrative strands, multiple ontologies, and uses a subjective realist style of narration to tell its story. Indeed, it is these key features that distinguish *Mulholland Drive*'s subjective realist multiform narrative from other styles of complex narratives used in the cinema. In this chapter, I will show how the use of the multiform narrative in *Mulholland Drive* parallels its use in films such as *The Cabinet of Dr. Caligari,* an early example of the style from the European art cinema. In doing so, I will demonstrate the usefulness of the subjective realist multiform cinema as a category, which in this instance allows for a productive comparison of two films separated by nearly a century. I will also demonstrate in the process that the roots of the style go deep into the history of cinema, back to the earliest instances of films with complex narratives.

On the continuum of narrative complexity, *Mulholland Drive* is arguably the most difficult of the key contemporary films under consideration here, and not surprisingly, it is also the least commercially successful. Stylistically, *Mulholland Drive* can be seen as providing a link between the European art cinema, where the subjective realist multiform narrative was developed, and the contemporary American independent cinema, from which "smart films" such as *Memento* and *Eternal Sunshine of the Spotless Mind* have emerged. In order to show the continuities between contemporary multiform cinema and its art cinema precursors, I will begin this chapter with a consideration of *Mulholland Drive*'s narrative and aesthetic similarities to two films from German silent cinema, *The Student of Prague* and *Caligari*, exploring the ways in which *Mulholland Drive*, like these early films, employs exhibitionistic aesthetic techniques in its subjective realist multiform narrative. My intention is to demonstrate that *Mulholland Drive*, like numerous other contemporary multiform films, uses a narrative style closely related to the styles developed in the avant-garde trajectory of the cinema of attractions (Gunning 1990: 61).

I will also present an analysis of the key critical work on *Mulholland Drive*, and the explanation I offer of the film is drawn from a growing consensus of commentators who view the film's first movement (and all its various strands) as a dream and its second as a waking frame that provides clues to making sense of the dream. I will argue that, although *Mulholland Drive* has affinities with the open-ended narratives of art cinema, its fragmented multiform plot structure does allow for a coherent narrative reading. *Mulholland Drive*, then, rather than providing an example of an experimental or incomprehensible narrative film, is rather an example of a hybrid: part exhibitionistic art cinema, and part classical Hollywood cinema. This hybridity is rooted in *Mulholland Drive*'s use of subjective realist narration in both its major strands, which are linked by unmarked ontological shifts. Here again, the subjective realist multiform cinema as a category provides a useful way of conceptualizing *Mulholland Drive*: it offers a way of articulating its narrative distinctiveness from mainstream Hollywood, while not overstating the degree of its narrative complexity (and/or incomprehensibility).

Finally, I will conclude with an analysis of the Club Silencio scene from *Mulholland Drive* that considers the ways in which exhibitionistic aesthetic forms are employed to both disrupt audience expectations as well to offer an implicit critique of Hollywood cinema. *Mulholland Drive*'s parody of the Hollywood dream and its critique of Hollywood narrative is a consistently commented upon theme in critical work on the film. Both of these themes are made explicit in the Silencio scene and will be considered in this concluding section, where *Mulholland Drive*'s theory of the cinema will be considered.

Expressionism and the Uncanny in *Mulholland Drive*

Novelist David Foster Wallace, in an article on David Lynch's *Lost Highway*, makes the following observation: "Since Lynch was originally trained as a painter (an Abstract-Expressionist painter at that), it seems curious that no film critics or scholars have ever treated his movies' clear relation to the classical Expressionist cinema tradition of Wiene, Kobe, early Lang, etc." (1997: 197). Wallace accurately identifies a gap in the critical work on Lynch, and I would like to briefly offer an analysis of *Mulholland Drive* that takes into consideration its links to Expressionism. I will examine the similarities between *Mulholland Drive* and several films from German silent cinema, including what is possibly the first multiform film, *The Cabinet of Dr. Caligari*. After exploring this relationship, I will argue that *Mulholland Drive* also shares with German Expressionism the exploitation of the magical possibilities of cinema described by Gunning as a characteristic feature of the cinema of attractions (1990: 58). I intend to show how contemporary multiform films such as *Mulholland Drive* can be seen in their relationship to both the cinema of attractions and the types of avant-garde cinema that it inspired.

German Expressionist cinema is a term applied to a highly stylized body of films made in Germany from 1919 to 1930. The Gothic mise-en-scène and acting styles employed in these films were directly influenced by the Expressionistic painting and theater of the era. These self-consciously artistic films were specifically targeted at international audiences, since, in the economically depressed period in which they were made, "Art ensured export, and export meant salvation" (Kracauer [1947] 2004: 65). Expressionist cinema is notable for its creation of "a self-contained fantasy world quite separate from everyday reality, a world imbued with angst and paranoia in the face of that which cannot be rationally explained" (Cook and Bernink 1999: 67). Expressionist filmmakers, in an effort to create a cinema distinct from commercial cinema yet still accessible to wide audiences, incorporated facets of the cinema of attractions into narrative feature films. Writing about the relationship between the cinema of attractions and early German cinema, Dietrich Schuenemann makes the following statement:

> Critics tend to understand the history of early cinema in its first decades as a move from the "cinema of attractions" to the narrative models and strategies of the "continuity style" of classical Hollywood cinema. German contributions from *The Student of Prague* and *The Golem* [Paul Wegener 1915] to *The Cabinet of Dr. Caligari*, *Nosferatu* [F.W. Murnau 1922] and *Metropolis* [Fritz Lang 1927] provide a different prospect. The attraction which cinema held in its first decade, the attraction of "making images seen," of "the visibility" of "real living moving scenes," was replaced by "the other." Cinema discovers, as a preview to *Nosferatu* highlights, the "tremendous attraction" which the presentation of the invisible, the uncanny and the eerie holds for the audience. And cinema discovers the suitability and great potential of its technological armature for the display of uncanny experiences. (2003: 13)

In Schuennemann's view, German Expressionist cinema can be seen as a part of what Gunning characterizes as the avant-garde trajectory of the cinema of attractions. It exploits the potential of the cinema for the display of magical and uncanny experiences. At the same time that Hollywood and other commercially oriented national cinemas were adopting narrative styles from the popular literature of the day, Expressionist cinema was building its narratives around the types of attractions present in the work of Méliès. Filmmakers like Lang and Weine did not eschew narrative like the surrealists would in the next decade, but they did seek to exploit cinema's potential to offer something different from commercial cinema by manipulating the visual and narrative elements of their films in ways similar to Méliès. Thomas Elsaesser writes: "We therefore ought to talk of the German Expressionist cinema as an art cinema, and it is here that the forms of the fantastic are developed, in the context of a self-conscious attempt to make 'art' in the cinema" (Elsaesser 1990: 32). As an art cinema consciously opposed to mainstream American, French, and German cinema of the day, Expressionism combined fantastic narrative forms with the techniques of attraction to create a new style of cinematic expression. I would argue that *Mulholland Drive*'s similarities to Expressionism, as well as to early German silent films like *The Student of Prague*, are not simply on the level of its self-conscious artfulness (its subjective realist multiform narrative, for instance), but also in its incorporation of the magical and uncanny into its narrative.

The Student of Prague—a film from a cycle of pre-Expressionist, romantically inflected German doppelgänger films—contains several narrative and aesthetic characteristics that were taken up by Expressionists and that are also evident in *Mulholland Drive*. *The Student of Prague* tells the story of Baldwin, a poor student who trades his mirror image to the mysterious Scapinelli for one hundred thousand pieces of gold. Baldwin subsequently finds himself haunted by this doppelgänger, who sabotages all of the expectations the money has given him by murdering the fiancé of a countess Baldwin is in love with. Ultimately, Baldwin meets an unhappy fate when, in an attempt to kill his double, he kills himself instead. The narrative similarities between *Mulholland Drive* and *The Student of Prague* are numerous: both are Cinderella stories that go wrong; both feature doppelgängers and a magic chain of causality; and both end with their central character killing him- or herself. *Mulholland Drive* recounts the story of Diane Selwyn, an ambitious young actress with hopes of achieving fame and fortune in Hollywood. Her hope is foiled by a love affair that ends badly and results in her descent into a murderous, psychotic rage that finally ends in suicide. Expressionist films often used a detection plot, the solution of which established "an identity between criminal and investigator, in other words, an explicitly Oedipal plot, which cannot but end in suicide or self-mutilation"

(Elsaesser 1990: 29). Doppelgängers, another common feature of Expressionist cinema, can be understood as the external manifestations of a part of the characters resulting from immense internal pressure and the characters' attempts to displace or transform the tension (Elsaesser 1990: 29). These attempts invariably fail and the doppelgängers turn on their creators, usually destroying them. Betty Elms, Diane Selwyn's oneiric double, is a clear variation on this theme.

Another important nexus with German silent cinema, however, can be seen in *Mulholland Drive*'s narrative affinities with Robert Weine's *The Cabinet of Dr. Caligari*, one of the most important films of German Expressionist cinema. *Caligari*, like *The Student of Prague* and *Mulholland Drive*, uses doubling and Oedipal plotting in its fantastic narrative, but, unlike *The Student of Prague*, it also features a multiform narrative: it has two strands and two distinct ontologies. It begins with Francis, the film's central character, telling a story to an unnamed man in the garden of an insane asylum and in this way introduces the spatial and temporal base of the film's diegesis. As Francis narrates his tale, however, there is a clear spatiotemporal (as well as, it is later learned, ontological) shift to the film's second strand—which features Francis's tale of the murderous Dr. Caligari and his somnambulist Cesare, as well as the parallel story involving a love triangle between Francis, his best friend Allan, and the woman they both love, Jane. Although the narration returns briefly to the first strand at the film's end, the majority of the action takes place in the embedded narrative that constitutes the film's second strand. That the film's narrator, Francis, is a patient in an asylum, and that his tale is ultimately unreliable are, of course, of no small significance. When Francis's mental illness is revealed, the major strand of the film is rendered delusional, much in the same way movement one of *Mulholland Drive* is when/if it is understood as a dream. Further, numerous questions regarding both Francis and the story he has told remain open at the close of the film: Is there any truth in his story? What is the cause of his insanity? Was Jane ever his fiancée? Was Allan really murdered, and if so, by whom? That these questions remain unanswerable demonstrates the film's opaqueness in regard to character motivation, and adds to the already complex narrative generated by its multiform structure and anachronic temporality. Elsaesser writes that one of the hallmarks of German cinema is "the manifest lack of unambiguous causal links between sequences," a trait that "invites symbolic interpretation" (1990: 29). Ambiguous causality is, for Bordwell, one of the primary characteristics of art cinema and has been seen by some as a central feature of *Mulholland Drive*. The unreliable narration of *Caligari* also provides a link to *Mulholland Drive*, since it is, in fact, this feature that motivates the use of a multiform narrative in both films.[1] Francis's tale, which is initially presented as a flashback, is later revealed to be the fabrication of a lunatic. Its ontological status as history is undermined by Francis's unreliability, much like Diane's dream is understood to be a fantasy in the oneiric reading of *Mulholland Drive*.

One further similarity between *Caligari* and *Mulholland Drive* is that both feature instances of fantastic narration in the Todorovian sense. In *Caligari*, the first of these takes place when Francis spends an evening spying on Caligari and Cesare, who he suspects of murder. As he watches, the narration shifts to a Cesare doppelgänger, who approaches the sleeping Jane and carries her away. When Francis hears of the abduction, he is shocked and cannot account for the doubling (just as the spectator cannot). The hesitation experienced by Francis (and the spectator) in relation to the Cesare double is one of several examples of fantastic events in the film. Others follow soon after this one, with the first taking place as Francis pursues Caligari to the asylum, where Francis suspects he might be a patient. Francis learns, however, that Caligari is not a patient, but the head doctor who has used his position to take advantage of Cesare's condition in order to commit a series of murders. The final twist of the film takes place when the narrative returns to the garden where Francis is telling his story and it is revealed that not only is he a patient, but so are Jane and Cesare, and the film ends with a deranged Francis attacking the head of the asylum, who is none other than Caligari himself. The effect of this final revelation is unsettling (and I would argue, disrupts the certainty that Francis's story is entirely untrue). The fantastic events of the film are, however, rendered comprehensible by the explanation that the narrator is mentally unstable—a common method of resolution in fantastic fiction, as Todorov's work shows. *Caligari*, like *Mulholland Drive*, is a fantastic-uncanny film in which (many or most of) the narrative's unexplainable events are ultimately explainable by laws of nature consistent with those of the everyday world. Both films provide examples of the ways in which narrative complexity function as a form of attraction: in both cases, the magical possibilities of the cinema are exploited to create temporarily unexplainable scenarios that are later revealed to be the result of unreliable (and/or restricted) narration. In addition, both films use subjective realism and multiform narration to create narratives more layered and complex than the average film. So, whether intentional or coincidental, then, *Mulholland Drive* has much in common with *Caligari* and with German Expressionism—one of the first of the avant-garde film movements to take up the aesthetics of attraction.

Three Views

I would now like to consider some of the critical work done on *Mulholland Drive*, while at the same time offering an analysis of its multiform structure and its subjective realist style of narration. *Mulholland Drive* is set in Hollywood and tells the story of Diane Selwyn (Naomi Watts), a bit-part actress overwhelmed by guilt after the murder of her former lover, Camilla Rhodes (Laura Elena Harring). The murder, spectators learn, is commissioned by Diane after Camilla ends their relationship and publicly humiliates her. The film has two major and several minor strands. The first of the major strands offers the film noir-inspired story of Betty Elms (also Naomi Watts), a talented young Canadian actress who comes to Hollywood in the hope of becoming a star. Betty immediately befriends the mysterious "Rita" (Harring), who is suffering from amnesia after a car accident on Mulholland Drive and the pair set out to discover the mystery of Rita's identity (as well as the question of where the ten thousand dollars they find in her purse might have come from). A number of minor narratives that feature characters loosely related to Betty and Rita are also woven into this first strand. In one of these, Adam Dresher (Justin Theroux) is a film director forced by mafia bosses to cast a woman of their choice in a leading role; in another, an incompetent thug commits a series of murders, apparently in an effort to locate Rita. The second major narrative strand begins with an unexplained shift in which the central character, Betty Elms, seems to be mysteriously transformed into another person: Diane Selwyn. This strand then presents Diane's final hours, made up primarily of a series of flashbacks (and hallucinations) that provide information regarding the events that have led to Camilla's murder, and eventually, to Diane's suicide. *Mulholland Drive* features not only a multi-strand narrative with alternate ontologies, but also numerous spatial, temporal, and causal disruptions. The central enigma posed by the plotting is the one of how these various strands fit together, or even if they fit together at all. There are a number of theories, as we shall see, and the competing explanations they offer will be considered.

The critical work on *Mulholland Drive* can be divided into three main categories: in the first, the film is understood to be incomprehensible; in the second, utterly comprehensible; and in the third, mostly comprehensible with varying degrees of incoherence (Andrews 2004: 25). The division of critical work into these three categories, as proposed by David Andrews, is immensely useful in gaining an understanding of the reception of the film. In recent years, the latter of these views has become dominant and is the position from which the film will be analyzed in this chapter—where it will be argued that *Mulholland Drive* does indeed have a coherent narrative and that many of its enigmas can be understood when it is read as an subjective realist multiform film. Its complexity results from the subjective realist narration employed to represent Diane Selwyn's dream in the first movement and her psychosis in the second. That the film is "mostly" coherent, however, is an important *caveat* since ultimately there are elements of the plot that remain enigmatic. In fact, *Mulholland Drive* is difficult to the point that many have viewed it as inscrutable. I do not think this is the case and part of my goal in this chapter is to demonstrate that, rather than being primarily an instance of a surrealist, experimental, or open-ended art film, *Mulholland Drive* can be understood as offering a coherent if fragmented story not dissimilar to the type often told by the Hollywood films it critiques. When the first movement of the film is understood as the subjective realist account of a dream, the film's multiform story becomes largely comprehensible.

As Surrealist or Trance Film

It is not surprising in the case of a complex film like *Mulholland Drive* that certain reviewers, critics, and scholars have understood it to be incomprehensible. David Bordwell, in his exploration of contemporary cinema, writes that "indeterminate movies are rare in American cinema . . . and perhaps, only David Lynch makes them" (2006: 82). Other examples of this view can be found in reviews of *Mulholland Drive* by Stanley Kauffman, Martha Nochimson, and Roger Ebert, all of whom believe the film to be intentionally indeterminate or finally unexplainable in narrative terms.[2] Yet, other reviewers have seen the film's narrative complexity as pretentious, or worse, as an example of poor filmmaking. Although I do not think these views are accurate, I do want to consider two particular critical readings that understand the film in these terms: Jennifer Hudson's "No Hay Banda" (2004) and Ruth Perlmutter's "Memories, Dreams, Screens" (2005). In considering these articles, I will focus on how the film is situated by these writers in relation to avant-garde cinema. Hudson and Perlmutter both understand *Mulholland Drive* as falling outside the bounds of narrative cinema, its plot too fragmented to make a coherent story from. In making their arguments, both writers align *Mulholland Drive* with avant-garde movements: in Hudson's work, it is argued to be surrealist, and in Perlmutter's, experimental.

Hudson's reading is primarily auteurist in its theoretical approach, and the central argument is that David Lynch's interest in the unexplained, combined with his "distrust of linguistic structure," provides the keys to understanding *Mulholland Drive*. Yet, Hudson adds, these keys have been ignored by most interpreters of the film, who consequently misunderstand it (2004: 170). If these matters are kept in focus, she argues, the film's "contradictions and meaninglessness" can be understood as intentional and the film can be seen as an attempt on the part of Lynch to blur "conceptual borders." "Like the blackness inside the film's enigmatic blue box, any logical nucleus for *Drive* remains elusive and indefinable. While audiences might try to perceive some trace of lucidity in the mirages of sound and vision that comprise the film, *Drive* remains a spiral, a circle, a series of unexplained pulsions that blur and destabilize traditional concepts of intellectual sense" (2004: 170). Hudson's argument, which is based primarily on statements made by Lynch in interviews, concludes by locating the film outside of the theoretical genre of narrative feature film. She argues that Lynch is a surrealist and that by extension, *Mulholland Drive* is a surrealist film. The disruptions of narrative coherence throughout the film are meant to frustrate spectators and the film is, finally, uninterpretable. (If *Mulholland Drive* is finally incoherent as argued by Hudson, then it certainly fits William Earle's description of surrealist cinema, where it is characterized by its retention of a recognizable background on which defamiliarized material can be foregrounded—disconnected from its everyday associations but still largely recognizable, even if ultimately incoherent.) Hudson's interpretation of *Mulholland Drive*, however, ignores even the possibility that many of the seemingly unexplainable elements of the film might actually be comprehensible or explainable.

In the oneiric explanation of *Mulholland Drive*, for instance, the first movement of the film is understood to be a dream, and the second, a fragmented and hallucinatory waking state. In this second movement, the viewer is offered a series of flashbacks that provide clues to unraveling of the mysteries introduced in the dream. In this explanation, there is indeed a "logical nucleus" to the film that renders it comprehensible, even if some of its strands remain difficult to finally make sense of. Hudson's "unexplained pulsions" can, in this account, be seen to result from the fact that the film is a subjective realist representation of the dreams and hallucinations of the psychotic Diane Selwyn. The oneiric view of the film renders its seeming incoherence as consonant more with ironic than surrealist cinema, as we shall see below, but it also provides an explanation for many of the mirages of sound and vision that comprise the film. What is important in regard to Hudson's reading, however, is the fact that the film is challenging enough to warrant such a reading. *Mulholland Drive*'s defamiliarization of the everyday is severe enough to allow for this view to be plausible, even if not finally persuasive.

Ruth Perlmutter also argues that *Mulholland Drive* is intentionally incoherent. However, where Hudson locates the impetus for the film's incomprehensibility in Lynch's desire to "destabilize traditional concepts of intellectual sense" (2004: 170), Perlmutter understands it to be motivated by an attempt to subvert traditional narrational norms and viewer expectations in a critique of the classical Hollywood style:

> To resist the dream factory's success at seduction and to challenge our need for coherence and identification with plausible characters, Lynch refuses to reconcile the two stories completely and endows them with the ambiguity of a dark trance-film, where nothing is real, everything is secondhand, or camouflaged by the artifice of Hollywood. To this end, the formal strategies of the film text frustrate our attempts at interpretation. The style, therefore, including the way it frays at the end and breaks down any sense of grounding in reality, is designed to cause some kind of anxiety in the viewer trying to make sense of it all. (2005: 132)

Like Hudson, Perlmutter understands the film as ultimately resistant to attempts to build a coherent story from the plot. She argues that the ambiguity of *Mulholland Drive* illustrates Lynch's "anti-cinematic thesis that film, already a doubling mechanism, is only a fake" (2005: 132). Perlmutter, however, unlike Hudson, does acknowledge in her article the possibility that an oneiric reading might offer a coherent account, but she finally resists this explanation.

Regardless of my disagreement with the explanations offered by Hudson and Perlmutter, what is relevant about their work is that both view *Mulholland Drive* primarily in terms of its resistance to the narrative conventions of Hollywood. *Mulholland Drive*'s formal characteristics—its subjective realism, its fragmentation (temporal, spatial, and ontological), and most importantly, its (seeming) lack of narrative closure—can be seen to resemble some of the most radical forms of art cinema. For these writers, *Mulholland Drive* constitutes an example of American counter-cinema, explicitly critical of Hollywood in its content and implicitly critical in its very form, much like the surrealist and experimental cinema it is compared to. This opens up the possibility that, unlike commercially driven mainstream Hollywood pictures, *Mulholland Drive* actually challenges dominant ideologies in ways that mainstream cinema simply cannot. The desire to situate *Mulholland Drive* in a place from which it can offer such a critique is, I believe, what drives critics like Hudson and Perlmutter to argue that the film is indeterminate. It is also a view regularly found in the work on films with complex narratives, which are often seen as subversive simply due to their formal characteristics. A close reading of *Mulholland Drive*, however, belies the view that the film is finally incoherent. (Whether or not this reading eliminates its critical impetus, however, is another matter.)

In regard to the arguments made in chapters 2 and 3, Hudson and Perlmutter's views could be translated as follows: *Mulholland Drive* is a complex and incoherent film. Its narrative complexity results from its unmarked ontological shifts, its subjective realist narration, its doppelgängers, and its unexplainable events. These traits make narrative recuperation impossible, and consequently, the film can be seen as closer to Earle's notion of Surrealist film than to either his Realist or Sensory film. In relation to Gunning's work, *Mulholland Drive* can be seen as employing an exhibitionistic style that employs attractions in ways that resemble their use in the Expressionist and surrealist cinema.

As Fragmented, Subjective Realist Film

At the other end of the spectrum from Hudson and Perlmutter are Jay R. Lentzner and Donald R. Ross, who argue that *Mulholland Drive* is *completely* coherent. Lentzner and Ross argue that if analysis of the film begins with the "recognition that its diabolically intricate form is a dream that obeys rules set forth a century earlier in Sigmund Freud's *The Interpretation of Dreams*," it can be rendered coherent (2005: 102). Lentzner and Ross's understanding that the numerous narrative disruptions in the film are the result of its representation of a dream is shared by numerous critics, yet the certainty with which they explain these is rather unique. Lentzner and Ross see *Mulholland Drive*'s first movement—which they refer to as "Part A"—as "the manifest dream content as experienced by the dreamer, Diane Selwyn" (2005: 103). "Part B" by contrast, "spans the final twenty minutes and presents fragments of her day residue along with both her pre- and postdream waking reveries, which are the keys to unlocking the dream's latent content" (2005: 103). Lentzner and Ross provide an account of many of the mysterious and seemingly unexplainable elements of the first movement by way of the clues provided in the second, and they use the rules "set forth by Freud" to do this (2005: 103). In contrast to Hudson and Perlmutter, Lentzner and Ross implicitly argue that the film *is* explainable in terms of the conventions of classical narrative realism; although *Mulholland Drive* is more complex than the average Hollywood film, once its shifts from one ontological framework to another are identified, its intricate structures become comprehensible. The formalist distinction between plot and story becomes important here. For Lentzner and Ross, the *story* of *Mulholland Drive* becomes as obvious as that of the *The Wizard of Oz*, as in each film, the bulk of the plot is simply the subjective realist representation of a dream. When the plot fragments are rearranged in their appropriate order, the stories told by the films are entirely comprehensible. In their framework, Diane's dream, like *all* others apparently, can be definitively interpreted using the tools provided by Freud, who understood dreams to be disguised wishes.

Lentzner and Ross argue that movement one "expresses [Diane's] latent fantasies and agonizing unconscious conflicts, which are disguised fulfillment of repressed wishes" (2005: 111). Their use of *The Interpretation of Dreams* offers them useful tools for interpreting *Mulholland Drive* and though it provides many interesting insights into the film, they are not always convincing. For example, Lentzner and Ross argue that the mystery of Rita's true identity is simple: she is a synthesis of Camilla—Diane's former lover—and Diane's mother (2005: 108). The synthesis takes place through the process Freud calls *condensation*, demonstrated in this instance by Diane's subconscious transformation of these two real-life counterparts into a single figure in her dream: Rita. This view of Rita also draws from Freud's work on female sexuality, particularly his thesis that lesbianism stems from a subject's inability to separate from the mother and to develop a "normal" erotic object choice (1937: 387). This explanation of Rita's true identity, however, while persuasive within a Freudian framework, has little basis in the textual evidence provided by the film. This seems to me a sticking point for a reading that purports to definitively interpret *Mulholland Drive*. My objection to their interpretation on this point is simply that the film itself offers no concrete information about Diane's mother. (Although some critics, including Lentzner and Ross, have seen the elderly couple Betty that exits the airport with in the early part of movement one as her parents, this interpretation is merely speculative.) The idea that Rita is a condensed version of Camilla and Diane's mother seems not to be based on evidence, but imposed by the interpretive framework itself.

Lentzner and Ross offer a slightly different explanation for the character Betty—Diane's alter ego in Part A. According to Lentzner and Ross, Betty is the result of *displacement*, a process in which the dreamer "shifts psychically intense elements in a dream away from their original sources onto objects more acceptable to the censoring ego" (2005: 108). Through displacement, Diane transforms herself into Betty, the ingénue who impresses casting agents and wins the love and affection of the helpless Rita. Displacement, then, provides explanations for the Betty/Diane doppelgängers as well as an explanation for the transformation of the unnamed blonde-haired woman at Adam Dresher's party (in the waking strand) into the talentless actress "Camilla Rhodes," whom Dresher is forced to cast as the lead actress in his film (in the dream strand). There are obvious reasons why condensation and displacement might be important processes for the sleeping Diane Selwyn, the mediocre actress who has paid a thug to kill her former lover—the talented, successful, and beautiful Camilla Rhodes. The truth, it seems, is simply too much for Diane to accept, making the need for these transformations necessary in the dream.

Day residue is the term that describes the daily experiences that the subconscious mind reconfigures into dreams, and Lentzner and Ross view the second part of *Mulholland Drive* as the residue of Diane's waking world, the stuff from which her dream is compiled. The second movement provides spectators with the true identities of the individuals in the dream, as well as the events and objects displaced and symbolized. Lentzner and Ross further explain the numerous examples of *symbolism* in the dream, which disguise and replace "unacceptable thoughts with less threatening visual images": Rita's amnesia and her link with Club Silencio serve to "associate her with death"; the enigmatic blue box represents female genitalia and also Diane's dream itself, as it captures "the paradox of its ultimate mystery and bottomless nature"; and finally, the blue key, which serves to confirm Camilla's murder in the second movement and becomes the source for unlocking the mystery of the dream itself—that is, the key is a symbol of the murder of Camilla, which is, of course, the theme that subtends the dream (Lentzner and Ross 2005: 109). Lentzner and Ross's account of many of the particulars of the film echo what has become the dominant explanation of the film, a reading that, for the most part, accounts for much of *Mulholland Drives*'s diabolically complex elements. Their identification of the ontological shift from movement one to movement two as the movement from a dream to a waking reality provides an immensely useful tool for understanding the film, and, if accepted, provides a very persuasive case for a coherent reading of *Mulholland Drive*. It also brings us closer to my own view of the film, which is that *Mulholland Drive* is coherent because it is a subjective realist multiform film. Movement one offers spectators a dream, represented from the point of view of Diane Selwyn, who is experiencing a brief respite from the horrors of her guilt-ridden waking life. The unexplainable elements of the movement (e.g., Rita's identity, the money, the blue box, the key, Diane's disappearance, the nature of the Terrifying Bum) can be understood as resulting from the fact that the narration represents the subjective realist perspective of Diane, who is dreaming. The ontological fragmentation is explained by recognizing that at the opening of movement two, Diane simply wakes up. However, in movement two, spectators are offered a temporally and spatially fragmented tour of Diane's rapidly deteriorating psyche. They are also provided with the day residue that has made up the dream itself. This much of Lentzner and Ross's explanation of the film works very well, and apart from their explanation of Rita, offers clear and persuasive explanations for the exhibitionistic aesthetic and narrative characteristics of the film. What makes many spectators resist this view that the film is coherent, however, is that it requires the acceptance of a very unpleasant idea: Betty Elms is simply not real. As a character in the dream of the murderous Diane Selwyn, Betty is merely a figment of an active and unstable imagination. To accept Diane Selwyn as the story's focalizer requires a disavowal of identification that is rarely demanded of spectators. For many, it is simply too much to ask. (In this sense, *Mulholland Drive* resembles *Memento*, which also requires spectators to radically revise their understanding of its central character.)

While the oneiric understanding of the film is largely followed here, Lentzner and Ross's notion that the film is entirely coherent is not. This is because at least some of the enigmas raised in the film do not seem to be resolved in the oneiric explanation, and although these are minor (as we shall see below), they undermine the certainty and definitive account of the film offered by Lentzner and Ross. Another particular difficulty with Lentzner and Ross's reading of the film has less to do with their explanation than with their interpretation, and this is particularly the case in their view of the Club Silencio sequence, which they rightly see as both pivotal and as an encapsulation of the main themes of the film. The conclusions they reach in their analysis, however, seem to me to be based on a fundamental interpretive error. They write: "There is no orchestra. It is all an elaborate fake. In the spine-tingling theater of the Club Silencio, the line between fantasy and reality blurs in much the same way as it does in the dream itself. . . . Freud was convinced that dreams, when rightly interpreted, represent communications of high import and definite meaning. This appears to be at variance with Lynch's nihilistic challenge to the distinction between fantasy and reality" (2005: 119–20). Lentzner and Ross's argument shifts here from a view of movement one as the dream of Diane Selwyn to an attribution of its content as a philosophical position that they attribute to the film's director. This is a rather dubious move. However, even if their analysis of the scene were accurate, it is not clear how it constitutes an example of nihilism, since the blurring of the distinction between fantasy and reality is not nihilism (nothing is true so anything goes) but psychosis (an impaired contact with reality). If, as Lentzner and Ross persuasively argue, *Mulholland Drive* offers spectators two distinct worlds—the first a dream, and the second the waking experience of a psychotic character—then the blurring of the distinction between fantasy and reality within the film logically follows. To argue that Lynch is offering Diane's point of view as his own philosophic position seems to miss the point. Or, to be more specific, it equates Lentzner and Ross's own questionable interpretation of the scene with what it believes to be the author's intentions.

A further problem with this view of the Silencio scene, already partly expressed, is the assumption that the blurring of the distinction between fantasy and reality is necessarily pathological. There is no doubt that in Diane's case, it is indicative of a serious psychological problem, and "Lynch" could have hardly made this point more obvious. However, there are other ways of understanding the troubled relationship between fantasy and reality in which their blurring together is not pathological (or nihilistic) but merely a fact of human noetic faculties. This, in fact, is a position taken by Todd McGowan (2004), who, although also employing a psychoanalytic framework in his analysis of *Mulholland Drive*, departs significantly from Lentzner and Ross at some crucial points. McGowan agrees with Lentzner and Ross's view that the first movement of *Mulholland Drive* represents a dream of Diane Selwyn and that the second provides clues to the content of the dream. However, McGowan considers the first movement representative of the type of fantasy that often underlies attempts to make sense of experience, and the second movement as representing the desire that drives it. This explanation of the film's two movements as being driven by two distinct forces, fantasy and desire, offers yet another illuminating perspective for understanding the film, as well as providing a sharp contrast to Lentzner and Ross's view that the intrusion of fantasy into reality somehow corrupts Diane's experience to the point that it is rendered meaningless. McGowan, in contrast to Lentzner and Ross, argues that Diane's reality is structurally dependent on fantasy, which follows from his view that fantasy provides the very frameworks necessary for interpreting experience. In the context of psychoanalytic theory, this seemingly radical point of distinction results from the poststructuralist-Lacanian inflection of McGowan's position, in which meaning is generated not by a priori frameworks that exist independently of experience but by narratives, mythologies, or fantasies that actually structure the experience of reality and provide the tools for interpreting it. This, of course, is at odds with the more scientific/rationalistic Freudianism of Lentzner and Ross.

McGowan's reading of *Mulholland Drive* emphasizes the role played by fantasy in Diane's attempt, via her dream, to rectify the fissures, fractures, and terrors of her life. These forces are, in turn, the result of the guilt she is experiencing as a result of the murder of Camilla. The narrative structure of the first movement illustrates "the role fantasy has in rendering experience coherent and meaningful," and McGowan argues that the conventionality of this movement—its linear, cause-effect sequence of events in a comprehensible spatial orientation—can be understood in relation to the role fantasy (rather than reality) plays in structuring experience (2004: 67). In *Mulholland Drive,* Diane's dream, and thus movement one itself, is structured much like a Hollywood narrative. Until its final scenes, it offers a highly coherent and largely conventional set of characters and events. McGowan argues that as a result, *Mulholland Drive* foregrounds the relationship between cinema and dream, emphasizing how the dream/fantasy structure of movement one results from the narrativizing of the fragmented events provided in movement two into a coherent, linear narrative, in which cause and effect function the way they can only in fantasy—in this case, a fantasy that resembles a film noir–style Hollywood film. By contrast, McGowan argues, "the world of desire in the second part of *Mulholland Drive* lacks even a sense of causal temporality. Events occur in a random order, without a clear narrative logic," and this demonstrates the disruptiveness and "atemporal logic" of desire (2004: 73). "In contrast to the second part of the film, the first part seems more real, more in keeping with our expectations concerning reality. But, ironically, this sense of reality results from the film's fantasmatic dimension rather than its realism. Whereas we usually contrast fantasy with reality, *Mulholland Drive* underlines the link between the two, thereby depicting the role of fantasy in providing reality with structure. In this way the film supports Jacques Lacan's claim that "everything we are allowed to approach by way of reality remains rooted in fantasy" (2004: 68). McGowan argues that, on the one hand, *Mulholland Drive* thematizes the importance of Hollywood in offering the type of fantasy that "sustains or supports our experience of reality" (2004: 68). On the other, he believes *Mulholland Drive* offers a critique of Hollywood based on its refusal to follow the logic of fantasy to its endpoint, which results in a denial rather than an affirmation of reality. To express this in different terms, *Mulholland Drive*'s subjective realism can be seen as being directly opposed to the transparent immediacy of classical realism, particularly when Club Silencio's magician, Bondar, offers spectators the dramatic and disruptive reminders that what they are watching is an illusion: "There is no band, it is all a tape recording." According to McGowan, *Mulholland Drive* critiques the immediate forms offered by Hollywood because of the way in which they function to mask reality. In this view, Diane is a victim of Hollywood on both levels of the narrative (in her waking life, her Hollywood fantasy of stardom has come to naught, and in her dream, it proves unsustainable), and *Mulholland Drive* becomes an example of the classical psychoanalytic critique of Hollywood cinema as fantasy (wish fulfillment).

Returning to narrative theory, the discrepancies between Lentzner and Ross's view of *Mulholland Drive* on the one hand and McGowan's on the other can be understood through the lens of the formalist distinction between plot and story. Lentzner and Ross's understanding is that the story is finally similar to the classical Hollywood story, not a radical departure from it. Once the complex temporal, spatial, and ontological fragments are assembled, the film can be seen for what it is: a subjective realist multiform film that is, finally, completely comprehensible. (This is not unlike the type of argument made time and again by David Bordwell regarding films with complex narratives.) McGowan, on the other hand, argues that *Mulholland Drive*, though mostly comprehensible, offers a critique of the classical Hollywood narrative in both its form and its content. Formally, *Mulholland Drive* demonstrates that the supposedly realistic classical narrative style of Hollywood cinema is actually rooted in fantasy rather than reality. The causal, temporal, and spatial coherence of movement one does not have its origins in reality, but rather is a self-referential illusion generated by the cinema. Its realism is just as much a fantasy as the type of film noir on which it is based. *Mulholland Drive*'s story, by contrast, is meant to shock spectators into awareness, to remind them of the mediated nature of the fictional world in which they are immersed and to warn them of the dangers of the quixotic world of Diane Selwyn, in which Hollywood narratives become frameworks for living (and even dreaming). McGowan, like Hudson and Perlmutter, wants to maintain the possibility that *Mulholland Drive* offers audiences something more than the average Hollywood film, that it offers a critique of the status quo as well as an aesthetic alternative to it, and yet that it does this in the context of a semicoherent narrative, rather than in a purely experimental or surrealistic film. Returning to my own argument in regard to *Mulholland Drive*, I would say that the position of Lentzner and Ross places the film on the conservative end of the complexity continuum, whereas McGowan's view fits more comfortably with the position I wish to explore now.

As Supernatural Film

In contrast to the view that *Mulholland Drive* is either completely coherent on the one hand, or incomprehensible on the other, scholars such as McGowan and David Andrews have come to understand the film to be complex but mostly coherent. This approach does not attempt to explain *all* of the enigmas raised in the film, but does allow for an understanding in which narrative sense can be made. In this explanation, *Mulholland*

Drive is contrasted with, for instance, Lynch's previous film *Lost Highway*, which may well be incoherent in a classical sense.

David Andrews sees *Mulholland Drive* as characterized by numerous narrative gaps but strongly rejects the idea that it is incoherent or chaotic. He argues that critics who see the film as illogical, lacking in continuity, or nonsensical are "wrong" and that the film "is replete not with logic but with logics which require viewers to hold multiple understandings in suspense, . . . it refuses to satisfy the viewer's urge for a monolithic storyline, for a narrative impelled by a univocal intention" (2004: 25). Regardless of this lack, *Mulholland Drive* has a "densely unified narrative" that coalesces on multiple viewings "into an organic psychonaturalistic account, a seemingly unitary interpretation that depends on the film's explicit oneiric structure" (2004: 25). Andrews describes the two key sections as *movements* (a strategy I have emulated), and like the psychoanalytic theorists above, he understands the first as representing a dream, and the second, a waking state. He reads *Mulholland Drive* through the lenses of what he sees as its three logical modes: the oneiric, the supernatural, and the musical, although for my purposes I will only consider the oneiric and the supernatural.[3]

The oneiric mode, as we have seen above, provides a plausible unitary reading of *Mulholland Drive*, and Andrews summarizes it this way: "The entire film takes place in a mental universe—Diane's head—including those scenes that involve neither Betty nor Diane" (e.g., the micronarratives) (2004: 26). This mode of analysis, used by Lentzner and Ross and McGowan, offers the viewer explanations for many of the film's particulars—psychological explanations for the dream, as well as for Diane's madness and suicide. Andrews writes that *Mulholland Drive* "may be viewed as a non-naturalistic film with an implied naturalistic narrative" (2004: 26). (Or, to put this in Todorovian terms, its seemingly unexplainable events are ultimately explainable naturalistically, as the products of a dreaming mind, making it an example of a fantastic-uncanny narrative.) Andrews offers a close reading of movement one and also makes a convincing case for the oneiric mode. He argues that the credit sequence, featuring the jitterbug contest, is from Diane's predream memories and constitutes the opening frame of the dream sequence. The jitterbug scenes are immediately followed by images of her bed, and a point-of-view shot of her head descending to the pillow and accompanied by the sound of sleeplike breathing. There is then a dissolve to the "Mulholland Dr." street sign, where, he argues, the dream begins. The end of the dream is framed similarly. Diane wakes up in her apartment (at the oneiric Cowboy's bequest: "Time to wake up, pretty girl"), thus ending the first movement. The second movement then chronicles, in a subjective realist style, Diane's hallucinogenic reveries. "Just as the first section is viewed from the dreamer's perspective and is thus unreliable, the second section is viewed from the perspective of a paranoid woman on the verge of madness and suicide—and is also unreliable . . . This is a tricky strategy . . . for the second section has two divergent psychological purposes: both to imply a set of credible, naturalistic explanations for the dream's content and to reveal the mental deterioration of a mind from within that mind. That is, the second section must at once feel real and unreal, reliable and unreliable" (2004: 30). In this view, which to me is highly persuasive, both of the film's major strands are subjective realist. Both limit the information offered to spectators to that of Diane's own experience (and so offer no objective level of narration). The appeal of the oneiric reading, then, is that it makes sense of so many of the film's puzzling elements. Regardless of this, Andrews cannot fully embrace the oneiric mode.

He argues that the oneiric reading "flattens out the film and dispenses with many of the qualities that make it Lynchian" (2004: 30). That is, it makes the film too easy, too mundane, too simplistic, but mostly, too naturalistic. His rejection of the oneiric mode is rooted in a desire similar to the one that has led to Hudson's and Perlmutter's views of the film. Each struggles against the possibility that the film *is* actually quite coherent and conventional. For Andrews, this struggle leads him to posit his second logical mode of interpreting the film: the supernatural. In many of Lynch's stories, argues Andrews, "dreams act as portals to other dimensions, supernatural ones as real as ours" and *Mulholland Drive* is no exception (2004: 32). "My view is that the crowning achievement of Lynch's opus must be a film that allows the possibility that the unconscious is a conduit to some legitimate alternative reality or that ontological alternatives of some sort exist" (2004: 33). Andrews sees this dimension of Lynch's work, in tandem with "a cinematic indeterminacy that defies monolithic explanation," as essentially Lynchian traits (2004: 33). And to make his case for a supernatural reading, Andrews offers several instances of interpretive difficulties that arise within the oneiric reading, most related to the micronarratives. For example, he notes that Diane is not the only sleeper in the first movement; there are several scenes that can be read as being enclosed not in Diane's dream, but in Rita's, including: "the chain of calls from Roque to the hitman, the scene at Winkies of The Man Who Dies of Fright; the scene of the Castigliane brothers, and several others" (2004: 33). Since all of these episodes follow Rita falling asleep, they could be considered to represent her dreams rather than those of Diane. (Of course, they could also be Rita's dreams within Diane's dream.)

Andrews also suggests that the Terrifying Bum—a character who frightens one of the film's minor characters to death—may not simply be a symbol of Diane's crime and product of her guilty conscience (a view that logically results from an oneiric reading), but may indeed exist independently of Diane. This view of the Terrifying Bum can be supported by the fact that Mephistophelian characters from Lynch's earlier films—such as *Twin Peaks*'s Bob, and *Lost Highway*'s Mystery Man—are (arguably) supernatural characters. Andrews posits that *Mulholland Drive*'s Terrifying Bum might actually "be the one doing it"—that is, might be a demonic being urging Diane to suicide by influencing her thoughts and dreams. On this view, he is an embodiment of evil rather than simply a symbol, and this possibility, along with the others considered above, leads Andrews to conclude with this: "There is no ideally closed reading of *Mulholland Drive*. Nor should there be, since neither the oneiric or supernatural reading can be given primacy; both are there; the viewer has to find a way to accept that, to tolerate it, and ideally, to enjoy it" (2004: 34). Andrews's case for a supernatural reading in the larger context of Lynch's work is plausible. However, since it does not offer any more explanatory power than the oneiric reading—whether the film's alternate realities are merely dreams or some tangible supernatural realm, their structural function is the same: they are embedded narratives with different ontological status to the real world of the second movement—the oneiric mode has proven much more widely appealing. The problems Andrews introduces and questions he raises regarding the micronarratives remain open, however. For instance, are any of the micronarratives meant to be understood as Rita's dreams rather than Diane's? If so, are they dreams within dreams? Questions like these, which seem impossible to answer, remain, and for this reason, Andrews's argument that there is no ideally closed reading of the film is a strong one. It also demonstrates, yet again, the resistance of many commentators on the film to accept a reading that seeks to make the film entirely coherent.

My own view on the matter is that *Mulholland Drive* is a subjective realist multiform film, and that the oneiric mode of interpretation that serves as the basis for this understanding is highly persuasive. It provides a way of understanding *Mulholland Drive* that does not diminish its formal complexity, its critical dimensions, or its truly horrifying aspects. Neither does this view diminish the pleasures the film offers or its status as art cinema. Indeed, of the three contemporary subjective realist multiform films under analysis here, *Mulholland Drive* has proven to be by far the most difficult for critics and scholars to agree upon, and, hence, it should be considered the most difficult of those under consideration. As such,

Mulholland Drive is the least difficult of the three films to categorize. It fits into the older, less complicated model of art cinema, a model that is troubled by films like *Memento* and *Eternal Sunshine*, as we shall see in the coming chapters. *Mulholland Drive* can also be seen as an example of the way in which multiform narrative has been employed in contemporary cinema, along with the aesthetics of attraction, to create surprising, innovative, and sometimes shocking films. In this way, it is clearly a part of the cinematic tradition that has taken up the attraction in an effort to offer audiences exciting film-viewing experiences.

It Is All an Illusion

To conclude my analysis of *Mulholland Drive*, I would now like to consider the Club Silencio scene, which occurs near the end of the film's first movement. This scene is pivotal in two key ways. First, it is the penultimate scene of the first movement, and the events it represents result in the transition out of the oneiric and into the waking strand. Second, it marks the point where the horrors of Diane's waking life can no longer be disguised, where reality intrudes on her dream, and thus intrudes on her attempts to maintain the illusion she has created there. The Club Silencio scene embodies, in form and content, the key themes of the film, which will be considered here not simply for their relevance to *Mulholland Drive*'s subjective realist multiform structure, but also for the way they directly address some of the wider themes of this book. *Mulholland Drive* will be considered for its own theoretical engagement with cinema, and it is during the Club Silencio scene that it offers a direct comment on the classical Hollywood style of realism.

The sequence under consideration takes place near the end of the first movement, and begins when Betty is awakened by Rita, who, during a nightmare, cries out in her sleep, "Silencio . . . No hay banda . . . No hay Orchestra." Upon awakening, Rita demands that Betty accompany her to Club Silencio, where she believes they will discover clues to help unlock the mystery of her identity. They arrive at the club during what proves to be the beginning of a performance by Bondar, a magician, who uncannily speaks the very same phrase that Rita uttered in her sleep: "There is no band." He adds: "It is a tape recording. This is all an illusion. And yet, we hear a band." As he speaks, the sound of a trumpet begins and a musician appears from behind a curtain playing a muted trumpet. When the musician removes the trumpet from his lips, however, the music continues, disrupting the expectations of spectators, both those within the theater where the performance is taking place and those watching the film. This disruption happens even though Bondar has clearly expressed the fact that the music is prerecorded. A similar disruption takes place shortly after this when the next performer, Rebekah Del Rio, collapses on stage during her moving rendition of Buddy Holly's "Crying." Once again, although the performance is disrupted, the song continues, demonstrating that it is a tape recording. Although spectators have been warned several times by this point that the music is prerecorded, its power to deceive is demonstrated once again. The scene seems explicitly designed to demonstrate the power of theatrical and cinematic conventions to create illusion. Spectators' habitual association of what is seen with what is heard, in this case the trumpet and the *chanteuse*, provides Bondar with the opportunity to surprise them repeatedly. The unconscious process of associating a sound with its supposed on-screen source is exploited to great effect, and the way in which it is exploited provides a textbook example of the way in which hypermediated aesthetic forms can be used to disrupt the illusions created in the cinema. Bondar's repeated reminder that what we are hearing is not live does not penetrate the unconscious association of what appears to be synchronous sound with its corresponding image. Spectators, even though reminded again and again that what they are seeing and hearing is an illusion, are still deceived by it, and this demonstration of the ability of conventions to deceive audiences can be understood on several levels.

On the first and most literal level, Bondar's statement that *it is all an illusion* can be understood as referring to: first, the music heard in the theater, e.g., the ominous diegetic score that begins as Betty and Rita enter the club (and seems to be nondiegetic); second, the stage music that precedes the trumpet (e.g., the clarinet and the trombone), as well as the trumpet itself; and, finally, "Llorando," the song Rebekah Del Rio lip-synchs before collapsing on stage. It is all recorded, a sonic illusion that seems real (live) but is not; or, that seems immediate but is actually mediated. The performance can be understood as a kind of magic show based on the manipulation of the distinction between prerecorded and live music to create a series of Brechtian alienation effects for the audience. Both sets of spectators, those in the audience with Betty and Diane and those in the cinema (or their living rooms) watching the film, share uncanny surprise at the discovery that the music is not live but prerecorded. On this level, the performance calls attention to the way sound is used in the theater to create coherence and an illusion of realism, which it then dramatically disrupts. The performance is exhibitionistic not simply in its use of techniques such as direct address, but also in the manner in which it calls attention to form. In disrupting sonic expectations, it defamiliarizes conventions and reminds spectators that what they are watching is illusory. The performance at Club Silencio, then, is an example of the low-budget theater of attractions.

On another level, *it is all an illusion* can be understood as referring to the film itself, and more specifically, to Diane's dream. That is, the *illusion* Bondar is referring to is actually the diegetic world that both Diane and spectators have been engaged with for the previous hour and three quarters. The story of Betty Elms and Rita is simply a dream, a fantasy that will end when the film returns to the real world, where Diane Selwyn is asleep in her bed. The performance is metaphorical, the product of a dream, and Bondar serves as a messenger alerting both Diane and spectators of its imminent end. This explanation is supported by the fact that before Bondar disappears from the stage, his pronouncements have a visceral effect on Betty, who shakes violently in fear. It is further supported by the fact that in the very next scene, Betty unexpectedly disappears just as Rita prepares to insert the blue key into the blue box, which has materialized in Betty's purse during the performance. When opened, the box becomes a portal into which Rita also disappears, thus ending the dream, and in the next shot, Diane is awakened by her neighbor/former roommate/former lover pounding on the door. Bondar's proclamation that *all is an illusion* can be understood on this level as referring to the entire first movement of the film, which is an illusion in the sense that it is merely a dream. The larger context for this level of explanation then is the multistranded structure of *Mulholland Drive*, with the dream representing its first major section.

The next several levels on which the scene can be understood are more speculative than the previous ones, and yet each seems in keeping with the themes of the film. The first of these is that Bondar's statement is a comment, not simply on Diane's dream, but on the whole of *Mulholland Drive*. The story it tells is an illusion. Movement two is just as illusory as movement one. Both are "recordings"—there is no band, no stage, no Betty, Rita, Diane, or Camilla; the whole story is a fiction, not just movement one. It is all an elaborate cinematic fantasy. This interpretation is closely related to the next, which sees Bondar's statement not simply in reference to *Mulholland Drive*, but to the medium of cinema as a whole, as an art form, as an institution, and in all of its individual manifestations. In this sense, Hollywood is the proverbial dream factory, manufacturing illusions for mass consumption. The manner in which the performances at Club Silencio disrupt the illusion created by synchronous sound represent the way in which *Mulholland Drive*, in its very form, disrupts the continuity style and classical Hollywood narration. Or to be even more specific, this scene can be seen to embody

Mulholland Drive's critique of the voyeuristic realism employed by Hollywood to generate the type of fantasy that has come to structure the dream world of the deluded Diane Selwyn.

It has already been noted that the sonic disruptions in the scene call attention to form in a manner that disrupts the expectations of spectators and shatters the coherence that prerecorded synchronized sound generally seeks to create. This makes the scene a clear example of the way exhibitionistic forms can be used to challenge the realist style of classical narration. Further, the theatricality of the scene, as well as its exhibitionistic direct address—which are justified by the literal theatrical nature of the performance—place spectators in a position like that described by Richard Rushton, one in which the desire for absorption enters a dialectic relationship with the recognition of the illusory nature of the diegesis. As such, the Club Silencio scene creates in spectators the tension Earle describes as characteristic of ironic cinema. The fact that it is self-consciously foregrounding not simply form (prerecorded music), but the way in which this form is used to create a realistic illusion, however, makes it an even more conspicuous example of its critique of Hollywood cinema. That Diane is a victim of Hollywood in both strands of the narrative seems to leave no question as to the position it constructs on the matter.[4]

In summary, Mulholland Drive uses a subjective realist style of narration that situates spectators very closely to its central character, whose grasp on reality seems tenuous at best. Exactly how the various strands fit together and exactly what they mean might be less certain; however, the view taken here is that the first movement of the film, which largely adheres to the conventions of the classical Hollywood style of narration, recounts a dream in which Diane seeks to escape the guilt she is experiencing as a result of her responsibility for the murder of her former lover, Camilla Rhodes. The conventional narration in this strand, though, eventually falls apart, as does Diane's attempt to escape into a Hollywood-style fantasy world. The disruptions of the classical style at the conclusion of movement one represent this failure, and Diane is ultimately forced out of the realm of fantasy and back to waking reality. The final scenes of the first movement offer both a direct commentary on the conventions of the Hollywood style of narration as well as a disruption of these conventions, making Mulholland Drive a film that engages theoretically with some of the matters I have been exploring in this book. Of primary interest, however, is its demonstration of the power of cinematic illusion and the use of exhibitionistic techniques to destabilize this illusion in a manner that both challenges the Hollywood style and offers spectators the types of narrative pleasures these challenges have been providing audiences of the art cinema for nearly a century.

The second movement of the film presents spectators with clues that assist in making sense of the first; however, the entire strand is filtered through Diane's paranoid and psychotic mind, and its numerous causal, temporal, spatial, and ontological disruptions follow directly from its pathological origins. On its own, movement two most closely resembles the seminarrative style of disjunctive surrealism featured in *Un Chien Andalou*. Ironically, this radically fragmented movement is an invaluable source of narrative information. The irony, of course, is that the second movement is actually grounded in the everyday world, while movement one is pure fantasy. The narrative of *Mulholland Drive* is designed to represent character psychology using a subjective realist style that places spectators in a similar psychic space to that of its central character. The difficulty spectators experience in their attempt to assemble a coherent story from the fragments of the second strand and the fantasy of the first are meant to mimic the effects of the trauma that Diane herself has experienced. The narration of *Mulholland Drive*, like that of *Caligari*, disrupts conventions in an attempt to surprise and shock audiences, and *Mulholland Drive* can, as such, be seen as a contemporary manifestation of the cinema of attractions. Its subjective realism and multiform narrative firmly situate it in the tradition I have called the subjective realist multiform cinema, and although it is often grouped with the narratively indeterminate films of international art cinema by critics, *Mulholland Drive* remains closely bound to complex smart films such as *Memento* and *Eternal Sunshine*, to which we turn now.

Notes

1. According to Sigfried Kracauer, the addition of the asylum scenes to the *Caligari* script by Lang (who was originally intended to direct the film), subverted the revolutionary and anti-authoritarian elements of the original, which was not multiform. In the case of *Caligari*, then, the effect of this addition can be seen to have neutered its critique (61–67).
2. Stanely Kauffman, "On Films: Sense and Sensibility," *New Republic*, 29 October 2001: 28; Roger Ebert, "Lost on Mulholland Drive," *Chicago Sun Times*, 16 April 2001; Martha Nochimson, "Review of *Mulholland Drive*," *Film Quarterly* 56:1 (2002): 37–45.
3. Andrews's account of the film's third logical mode offers the possibility that the purposeful subversion of narrative determinacy is in the service of a musical or symphonic cinema, one more concerned with the sensuous, evocative, and emotional qualities of the medium rather than its narrative capabilities. This view places the film in relationship to experimental cinema, an echo of Hudson and Perlmutter, but

is overshadowed in Andrews's work by his arguments for oneiric and supernatural readings. However, it should be noted that a further exploration of these sensory and affective dimensions of the film, and of multiform cinema in general, would make for interesting further study.

4. There is, of course, one other manner in which Bondar's statement can be interpreted, and it is one that has already been mentioned above in the section on Lentzner and Ross's Freudian analysis of the film, which see the statement *all is an illusion* not as a comment on cinema, but as regarding "reality" itself. The idea that the world is an illusion is, of course, a common belief, and a basic philosophical/religious tenet of some systems of thought. Lentzner and Ross read the statement on this level, and see it as representing the nihilistic philosophical position of David Lynch. As I have already stated, the unwillingness, or even inability, to distinguish between fantasy and reality is not nihilism, nor does the possibility of its being interpreted on this level necessarily mean this represents the view of the director.

Chapter 5

MEMENTO

Memento, like *Mulholland Drive*, uses a multi-stranded narrative with alternate ontologies and a subjective realist narrative to represent the experience of its central character, Leonard Shelby (Guy Pearce). As such, it is a clear example of a subjective realist multiform film. *Memento*, however, has proven interesting to scholars primarily for its innovative temporality, which moves backward rather than forward in time. Although my analysis of *Memento* will consider this aspect of its complex narrative, it will be primarily focused on the film's multiform structure, and I will argue that situating *Memento*'s narrative in the category of the subjective realist multiform provides a way of articulating its uniqueness in a manner that distinguishes it from a number of other styles of complex narrative film.

The chapter will explore three key aspects of the film: its lying flashbacks, its restricted narration, and its temporally fragmented narrative. Although these strategies are interrelated, I will consider each separately, and in the first section, it will be argued that Leonard's unreliable account of his past and the series of lying flashbacks that accompany this account generate the alternate ontological narrative strands that make *Memento* a multiform film. In this sense, *Memento*'s complexity can be understood as a part of the tradition of narrative films stretching back to *The Cabinet of Dr. Caligari* in which ontological fragmentation and subjective realist narration are used to mislead spectators into making false assumptions about the character and/or the story told. The next section will consider *Memento*'s use of a highly restricted style of narration, which limits spectators' knowledge to only that possessed by the amnesiac Leonard. The use of restricted narration will be shown to work in tandem with the film's lying flashbacks to situate spectators in a position where close alignment with Leonard Shelby, *Memento*'s central character, is inescapable. The third section, which is closely related to the second, will explore the ways in which the narrative structure of the film is designed to place spectators in an epistemological conundrum similar to that of the pathological Leonard. This section will focus on *Memento*'s progressive-analeptic temporality and consider the way in which it is used to simulate Leonard's amnesia, itself brought on by a traumatic event that has affected his ability to rightly make sense of the world. This chapter will demonstrate that *Memento*, like *Mulholland Drive*, employs a subjective realist multiform narrative to represent the complex story of its central character.

Memento recounts the story of Leonard Shelby, a former insurance claims adjuster suffering from anterograde amnesia, a condition that makes forming new memories impossible. Although he can remember his life before the injury that caused the condition, he can remember nothing since. Leonard is driven by a desire for revenge after the supposed rape and murder of his wife, which he claims took place during a burglary of his home—and during which, he claims, he sustained the head injury that caused his amnesia. The narrative action is propelled by Leonard's motivation to find and kill the man responsible, and he views himself as a type of hard-boiled detective, combing through the facts of the crime to locate the murderer. His amnesia complicates his quest, but Leonard seeks to compensate through a system of notes, Polaroid photographs, and the tattooing of "facts" on various parts of his body. This system is meant to act as a substitute for his (absent) short-term memory; however, it proves to be highly unreliable, as does Leonard's account of his past and the narration that represents this account. The unreliability of Leonard's version of events is at the center of my argument, as it is the constitutive dimension of the film's multiform narrative, since what is initially presented as flashback is ultimately revealed to be fiction. *Memento*'s lying flashbacks are one of two key strategies that combine to create the film's uniqueness; the other is the innovative temporality of the main strand, which begins at the end of the story and works backward, scene by scene. This latter strategy creates for spectators a disorienting experience that, although not identical to Leonard's anterograde amnesia, produces a similar effect on the attempt to make meaning. *Memento*'s temporality re-creates the epistemological consequences of anterograde amnesia: like Leonard, spectators are continuously uncertain about where he is, why he is there, and how he got there. The narration of *Memento* situates spectators in a position of knowledgeability similar to that of Leonard: like him, they are denied access to prior events and, as a result, are unable to establish clear cause-effect connections between them. This epistemological conundrum is sustained until the film's penultimate scene, where the final pieces of the puzzle are provided, resulting in a radical disruption of the spectator's expectations.

The Four Strands

Memento has four distinct narrative strands: the first and primary strand provides an account of the murder of Teddy, a corrupt cop who takes advantage of Leonard's condition (by using him to kill a drug dealer and extort ten thousand dollars); the second chronicles a series of phone calls that take place between Leonard and Teddy just before Teddy's murder; and the third and fourth are presented as flashbacks that seemingly provide information about Leonard's past.

The first strand—which I will refer to as the progressive-analeptic strand—follows Leonard from the murder of Teddy backward in time to the point where he makes the decision to commit the murder. The decision is made after Leonard has killed the drug dealer Jimmy Grants and as a result of Teddy accusing Leonard of having killed his own wife. The story spans a period of several days and includes Leonard's interactions with Grants's lover, Nathalie (Carrie-Anne Moss), who also takes advantage of Leonard in order to protect herself from drug suppliers looking to collect the money Teddy has stolen. It also includes a number of interactions between Leonard and Teddy that (falsely) lead spectators to believe that Teddy might in fact be the murderer of Leonard's wife.

The second strand uses black-and-white photography to indicate its temporal difference from the first strand (it takes place before the murder of Teddy). In this strand, Leonard is shown in his hotel room talking on the phone to an unknown interlocutor, and the voice-over is often, though not always, accompanied by a visual representation of the events Leonard recounts. It is broken into segments and presented intermittently throughout the film, providing a noir-like voice-over narration,[1] diegetically disguised as a phone conversation with the interlocutor acting "as a surrogate for the audience" (Turbett 2001: 4). It is during these black-and-white scenes that spectators are provided important background information, including an account of the burglary, an explanation of Leonard's condition, the system he has employed to help him find his wife's murderer, and the story of the amnesiac Sammy Jankis (Stephan Tobolowski). Spectators also discover (along with Leonard) some of the numerous tattoos he has, including one of his latest, which reads, "Never

Answer the Phone." (Upon its discovery, Leonard, who has been openly relating his story over the phone line, quickly hangs up. He later confides in Teddy his suspicion that he may have been talking to someone trying to manipulate him into murdering the wrong person.[2] His interlocutor in the black-and-white strand is, of course, none other than Teddy, who is indeed manipulating Leonard in this manner.) Structurally, the fragmented black-and-white strand punctuates the reverse-sequenced unfolding of the main narrative strand of the film: after each of the main strand's episodes, a black-and-white scene from the hotel room is shown. The cutaways to the black-and-white strand provide spectators with a linear and, consequently, more stable space-time with which to orient themselves, as well as providing Leonard's backstory via the phone conversation. With respect to chronology, the black-and-white strand takes place immediately before the events of the main strand: it is immediately after Leonard hangs up the phone near the end of the black-and-white strand that his decision to murder Teddy takes place. That is to say, it is the earliest scene of the film—excluding the "flashbacks"—to which we now turn.

The first of the flashback strands, the Sammy Jankis Story, is embedded in the black-and-white strand and is presented episodically. It has a sepia-toned black-and-white coloration that distinguishes it from both the main strand and the black-and-white strand, and it is (supposedly) based on Leonard's dealings, as the representative of an insurance company, with a man named Sammy Jankis, who also suffered from anterograde amnesia. According to Leonard's account, Sammy sustained a minor head injury in a car accident that led to his amnesia. Leonard was assigned the task of investigating Sammy's wife's insurance claim and determined, through rigorous evaluation, that Sammy's amnesia was psychological rather than physiological: he should have been able to make new memories. Since he was not, the insurance company took no financial responsibility. As a result, Leonard was promoted, and Sammy's wife (Harriet Sansom Harris) committed suicide, exploiting Sammy's amnesia to have him administer multiple and ultimately fatal doses of insulin. The story acts as a kind of mantra for Leonard, who uses it to illustrate and reinforce what he believes to be the crucial difference between Sammy and himself. He says: "Conditioning didn't work for Sammy, but it works for me. I live the way Sammy couldn't. Habit and routine make my life possible." Leonard believes that his "system" has enabled him to function successfully. However, the spectator, who is initially convinced by Leonard's certainty, eventually realizes that his system does not work at all. In addition, spectators are ultimately led to suspect that the originating event of his trauma—the murder of his wife by an intruder—might well be untrue as well. This possibility is introduced through various visual clues throughout the film, as well as more overtly when, near the end of the film, Teddy claims that it was Leonard not Sammy who gave his wife an overdose of insulin. If this is true (and I will argue that it is), the version of the Sammy Jankis Story embedded in the film is indeed fictional in regard to the main diegesis.

The second subjective realist strand, the Trauma Narrative, provides information about Leonard's relationship with his wife (Jorja Fox) and the burglary during which she is supposedly raped and killed. This strand is less a fully developed narrative than a group of short visual fragments. Included are several soft focus shots of Leonard's wife in a domestic setting; others in which Leonard interacts with her in their bedroom; and finally, a few violent scenes of the burglary itself. In several of these scenes, Leonard's spoken account of the events is undermined by images that contradict it. For example, in the flashbacks to the burglary, it is evident that Leonard's wife survived the attack, as in two separate sequences, she is seen alive even though he indicates she was not (in one, she is breathing, and in another, she blinks her eyes). The contrast between his spoken account—as he tells the story to Teddy in their phone conversation—and the visual representation is a clear indication that Leonard is intentionally lying, or, at least, withholding some important details. These visual clues lend credence to Teddy's version of the story later in the film, which holds that Leonard's wife was not, in fact, killed in the attack but died later as the result of an insulin overdose administered by Leonard himself. Another flashback strongly reinforces this possibility and takes place while Leonard attempts to watch television at Natalie's house. In this one brief shot, spectators are presented with what appears to be a flashback of Leonard preparing a syringe. What it suggests is: first, that Leonard's wife may have indeed had diabetes, and second, that the Sammy Jankis Story may actually be the Leonard Shelby Story, just as Teddy alleges.

Unreliable Narration

The difficulty of making a story out of *Memento*'s fragmented narrative stems not simply from its reverse-plotting and multiple temporalities, but also from what I see as its mixed ontology. The Sammy Jankis Story and the Trauma Narrative, both presented as flashbacks and framed through Leonard's acts of remembering, are not, in fact, flashbacks. Both, as I have already begun to argue, are actually lying flashbacks in which spectators are offered what seem to be memories but what are actually fabrications dreamt up by Leonard to protect himself from the truth of his past. This is an important structural distinction since, if they were actual flashbacks, the film would simply be a temporally fragmented multi-strand narrative rather than an subjective realist multiform narrative.

Leonard's credibility as a narrator—and consequently the ontological status of his (verbal) account of the burglary—is undermined by the numerous occasions in the main narrative strand where he revises "facts" regarding various matters to suit his purposes. These revisions take place at several points, but most importantly, in his false identification of Teddy as John G., his wife's supposed murderer. In addition to the clear cases in which Leonard falsifies the facts, there is also Teddy's account of the past, which flatly contradicts Leonard's. If Teddy's version of events is true—and the fact that Leonard lies to himself on several occasions certainly makes it seem more likely—then it was Leonard himself who revised the police report of the burglary. Further, Leonard's "memories" of Sammy Jankis are distortions, probably based on his own story. (Consider the scene late in the film where Sammy is shown sitting in a psychiatric hospital: a doctor walks past and, for a split second, it is Leonard and not Sammy sitting in the chair.) Leonard's revisions weaken not only his credibility as a narrator, but the very basis of his identity. Is Leonard who he says he is? Was his wife really killed by burglars? Could Leonard actually be Sammy Jankis? Teddy's account answers some of these questions, but Teddy is also open to suspicion since he has clearly been manipulating Leonard for his own purposes. His revelation could simply be part of his plan to keep using Leonard to do his dirty work. If this is the case, then spectators are left with a large set of unanswered and finally unanswerable questions.

The visual contradictions of Leonard's story, combined with Teddy's version of the past, however, provide sufficient evidence to conclude that it was indeed Leonard who (mistakenly) killed his wife. In my view, Teddy's account does provide an objective basis to counter Leonard's version of events, and *Memento*, like *Mulholland Drive*, can be understood as presenting a largely comprehensible story. This is not to say that the narrative is *wholly* explainable, but more that its complex plot can be assembled into a coherent set of events in a logical cause-and-effect sequence. This is particularly true of the events surrounding the murder of Teddy, but much less so regarding Leonard's past.

Disrupted Expectations

Undoubtedly the most surprising moment in *Memento* takes place late in the film when it is revealed that the shooting of Teddy during the film's opening sequence is not the justified revenge killing of the man who has raped and murdered Leonard's wife but a premeditated, cold-blooded murder resulting from Leonard's willful distortion of facts and conscious act of self-deception. Spectators, who until this point in the narrative had been aligned closely with Leonard, may understandably experience a powerful shock when it is revealed that Leonard, rather than being a wronged man seeking vengeance for the murder of his wife, is actually more akin to a serial killer. The force of this disruption is derived from the manner in which the narration so thoroughly aligns spectators with Leonard's perspective. Spectators, who have identified with the seemingly sympathetic Leonard, are faced with the possibility that he is not, in fact, sympathetic after all. This disruption of identification also offers yet another point of similarity to *Mulholland Drive*, where the oneiric reading requires a similar re-evaluation of its central character. Leonard, like Diane Selwyn, is a murderer, and the acceptance of this is challenging to spectators of both films.

In order to achieve the film's twist, the narration of *Memento* creates a close spectatorial identification with Leonard in his quest to avenge the death of his wife. Dion Turbett writes:

> The combination of voice-over narration, monologues (via the telephone) and soliloquies that spill out from the self-contained black and white space of the motel room have a two-fold effect: it more greatly presents the world through Leonard's subjectivity where his mind permeates every element of the film world (a direct relation to the film's structure); and it more generally encourages character identification (in that through these diverse modes of address Leonard attempts to order his world and this ordering, which places Leonard at its centre, continually strengthens the bond between the audience and him). (2001: 4)

Leonard's confidence in his own identity and the justness of his quest become the narrative cornerstones of the film. The bond forged between Leonard and spectators, coupled with the highly limited information provided, leaves spectators with little choice but to believe Leonard's account of the rape and murder of his wife, and, consequently, to feel sympathetic to his quest for vengeance. It is understandable, then, that spectators expect to learn that the murder of Teddy in the film's opening sequence is justified: that Teddy must be the "John G." that Leonard has been seeking. The revelation of Leonard's true motives for killing Teddy in the final sequence of the film, then, is highly disturbing to spectators, who have been positioned to believe Leonard's story and to identify with him in his quest. As a result, spectators are forced to re-evaluate their view of Leonard and may, at this point, seek to distance themselves from him.[3] The effect is upsetting for spectators so conditioned to siding with protagonists like Leonard, who are supposedly out to right the wrongs visited on an innocent loved one. The rupturing of identification is yet another example of *Memento*'s use of an exhibitionistic narrative style. In this example, *Memento* uses a radical disruption of narrative conventions to create its affect. It is an exhibitionistic moment that foregrounds form, and it can be argued that this subversion of expectations forces spectators into an awareness of the conventions the film is subverting as they seek to assemble a story from the radically fragmented plot.

The use of a highly restricted form of narration, which limits spectators' knowledge to only that which is known by its self-deceived amnesiac narrator, situates them in a relationship to Leonard that becomes uncomfortable when his decision to murder Teddy comes to light. It also means that the twist that follows from the revelation that the murder of Teddy is cold-blooded is different from the twists of other similar films. In *Fight Club*, for example, the revelation that Tyler and Jack are the same person initially seems impossible, as does the disappearance of Diane in *Mulholland Drive*. *Memento*, by contrast, never leaves the naturalistic world. Its uncanny moment is derived from its tightly limited flow of information, rather than any unexplainable or seemingly supernatural events. The disruption is possible because of the manner in which the conventions of a well-known story pattern, the rape-revenge narrative, are subverted.

Subjective Realism

The most unconventional aspect of *Memento* is, of course, the progressive-analeptic temporality of its main strand. This innovative structure provided spectators with a new kind of cinematic experience, and has, not surprisingly, been much written about. I want to take some time now to consider this aspect of *Memento* and particularly its relationship to the subjective realist dimension of the film. William G. Little has likened the experience of watching *Memento* to living through a trauma, arguing that the effect is both shocking and disorienting. In addition, he writes, "the film might be said to bear marks of traumatic experience" (2005: 68).[4] *Memento*'s narrative structure is motivated by its subjective realist style. The film reflects, in its very structure, Leonard's psychological disorder. Given this, it is not surprising that trauma theory is drawn on by scholars such as Little to assist in explaining the film. Little, for example, explores the relationship between *Memento*'s narrative repetitions and unanswerable questions through the lens of trauma theory, arguing that the narrative strategy employed in *Memento*—designed to mimic the effects of Leonard's condition, including his inability to accurately narrate his experience—makes it impossible for spectators to get a satisfying answer to the film's most conspicuous question: Who is Leonard? Spectators are placed in a philosophical conundrum similar to the one faced by Leonard himself (and one common to many victims of trauma): the inability to make a coherent story out of the available data. Further, as Leonard is the source of the majority of narrative information provided to spectators and the veracity of his account is severely undermined by his condition (as well as by his willful distortion of the truth), it is debatable whether the spectator can really answer the question of who he is. Teddy, the other key source of information in the film, may also be unreliable, which means that ultimately, *Memento* places the spectator in the role of detective, who must make sense of the series of seemingly unanswerable questions raised above. That many of these questions are left unresolved is, according to Little, one of the ways in which the narrative structure of the film mimics the effects of trauma. The source of Leonard's amnesia may have been the blow to his head, or it may have been the result of his wife's death; there is no definitive cause in the film. Whether physical or psychological, however, his amnesia is clearly the result of trauma, and one of the common effects is the inability of victims to re-present the trauma in a coherent manner (that is, to fit the experience into a coherent narrative). The link to Janet Murray's violence-hub narrative is clear here. *Memento* is a film in which a violent (and ambiguous) event—the burglary of Leonard's house—sits at the center of a set of narratives, each of which tries to make sense of it but none of which are successful. The narrative structure of the film is, then, in a very real sense, symptomatic of Leonard's inability to understand his past.

Of Leonard's many symptoms, his compulsion to repeat certain behaviors can be seen as a way in which he seeks to make sense of the world. What these repetitions ultimately become symptomatic of, however, is his inability to do so. This is never more evident than in the scene where Leonard hires a prostitute to assist in the re-enactment of the night of the burglary. He asks her to arrange his wife's belongings around the hotel room and then wake him up by slamming the bathroom door. Although she does what he asks, it proves to be an exercise in futility. He sends her away disappointedly and burns the mementos. Shortly after this scene with the prostitute, he asks: "How am I supposed to heal if I can't feel time?" This question seems to encapsulate the dilemma that the failed re-enactment represents. The spectator is placed in a similar relationship with Leonard's past and is left with a similar question: How am I to make sense of this story if I am not provided a clear chain of causality in a coherent temporality?

Leonard's multiple tattoos are also evidence of his struggle to make sense of his experience and Little argues that Leonard "is replaying the original trauma on the field of his body" (Little 2005: 73). Leonard's body becomes a living memento, an object tied to his search for authentic experience. Tattoos (falsely) promise Leonard a stable frame of reference, a way of remembering what he would ordinarily forget: He says, "If you have a piece of information which is vital, writing on your body instead of on a piece of paper can be the answer. It is just a permanent way of keeping a note." Little sees Leonard's repeated tattooing as a means by which he seeks to write a seamless autobiography, one that erases all of his compromising and traumatizing frailties (2005: 83). His tattoos become a way for him to narrativize the trauma that he cannot remember: *John G. Raped and Murdered My Wife*. They give his life purpose: *Find Him and Kill Him*. And they provide him with clear instructions as to how to achieve this purpose: *Photograph Car, Hotel, Friends, Enemies; Do Not Trust Anyone*. Unfortunately for Leonard, like the other repetitive behaviors that characterize his attempt to condition himself, this one fails as well. His tattoos become emblematic not of the authenticity he seeks but of the unreliability of his system, and of his murderous self-deceptions. The repetitive nature of the tattooing, like Leonard's other repetitive behaviors, also reflects the way in which the narrative structure of the film mirrors Leonard's experience of the world. And, the connection between narrative form and subjective realism is a crucial characteristic not just of *Memento*, but of subjective realist multiform cinema in general, as we have seen. *Mulholland Drive*'s structure mimics the subjective reality of its central character, as do those of films such as *Caligari, Wild Strawberries*, and *Eternal Sunshine*.

In another article that explores the manner in which *Memento*'s form is seen to embody the trauma it seeks to represent, Peter Thomas draws on contemporary literary and cinematic narrative forms more generally, focusing on the theory that trauma is not encoded in the same way normal memory is but rather is dissociated, fragmented, and repressed (2003: 205). Thomas associates the fragmented and dissociative type of memory produced by trauma with modernist and postmodernist narrative aesthetics and argues that the narrative corollary to traumatic memory in *Memento* is its progressive-analeptic structure, which, as mentioned above, effectively inverts cause and effect, placing the spectator in a position that is epistemologically similar to that of Leonard. Like him, spectators are unable to construct a coherent narrative out of the fragments since they are situated in a position from which it is nearly impossible not to misinterpret what is taking place. Leonard, for his part, denies the possibility that his interpretation might be compromised by his condition, and early in the film he denigrates the importance of memory: "Memory is unreliable. No really. Memory is not perfect. It's not even that good. Memories can be changed or distorted and they are irrelevant if you have the facts." In Thomas's reading of *Memento*, Leonard is like the historian facing a past he has not lived and without an adequate set of facts. The problem for Leonard is constructing a reliable or coherent narrative. "Leonard's need for textual fragments to gain some access to the past allows the film to externalize the making, revision, and distortion of memory [as well as] concretizing his revision of memory" (Thomas 2003: 205). Leonard's willful distortion of the few facts available to him and, by extension, his willful self-deception, proves that his system cannot work. Thomas argues that Teddy's revelation is true—Leonard has killed his wife by giving her an overdose of insulin—and that this is the real trauma that has shaped Leonard's quest. He then considers what this means for the spectator:

> Seen this way, the film seems designed to implicate the audience emotionally in an exploration of the process of constructing a cause-and-effect chain from fragmentary clues, in order to bestow meaning and dispel the painful ambiguity of an unavailable past, lost somewhere behind a wall of texts. *Memento*'s manipulative use of a highly suppressive narrative and the extreme emotional proximity it constructs with Leonard has constantly tempted the viewer to jump to retrospectively regrettable conclusions. In this way, what is stressed is the place of the reader's own desire in the unavoidable gamble of interpretation. (Thomas 2003: 207)

Thomas argues that the disruption of the conventions of the rape-revenge scenario and the shocking revelation that it was actually Leonard who killed his wife shatters "the already damaged Manichean framework that the audience initially shared with Leonard, and reveals the hidden will to identify, and identify with, pure victimhood" (2003: 207). The idea that the film exposes the desire of the spectator to identify with victimhood is bound up in the pleasure this identification offers when vengeance is exacted on the victimizers. This pleasure, common in Hollywood cinema, is ultimately denied by *Memento*. Thomas's view of how identification works in the film seems to me more defensible than Turbett's (and certainly fits with my own experience watching the film). Thomas's reading also foregrounds the way in which this subversion of the rape-revenge narrative can be seen as critical of the ideologies so often embedded in it.

The exploitation of spectators' will to identify with victimhood actually serves as the basis of an argument made by David Martin-Jones, who holds that *Memento* does this in the service of a critique of the American national narrative of triumphalism, one that often employs the rape-revenge narrative as a means of establishing its legitimacy.[5] Martin-Jones's argument regarding *Memento* also begins with the assumption that it was, in fact, Leonard who killed his wife, and that his amnesia is his way of hiding this fact from himself. Leonard's forgetting makes possible the creation of a false origin, which then serves as the basis for his revenge narrative. The false origin of Leonard's trauma, in turn, becomes for Martin-Jones an allegorical representation of the types of narratives used to justify American military intervention in places like Iraq, where false origins are posited in order to falsify motives and preserve the illusion of just cause. Martin-Jones focuses on the importance of this strategy in both narratives of American national identity and in American popular culture. "The triumphal narrative asserts that American military triumph is inevitable because it is America's destiny. This notion is drawn from the nineteenth century idea of Manifest Destiny, in which the supposed right of Europeans to conquer the New World was coded as inevitable, thereby eliding the reality of their colonial actions. Moreover, in the triumphal narrative American military victory is coded as righteous, as an action only committed once provoked" (2006 122–23). Martin-Jones demonstrates how this works in the cinema via a consideration of the overt triumphalism of *Saving Private Ryan*, which he sees as a reiteration of American triumphalism in its suturing over the U.S. military failure in Vietnam by borrowing sentiment from the recent U.S. military victory in Kuwait, using World War II as its setting. In Martin-Jones's reading, *Saving Private Ryan* becomes the embodiment of George H.W. Bush's statement: "By God, we've kicked the Vietnam syndrome once and for all" (2006 122). *Memento*, on the other hand, is seen to "critique this use of the past to establish false origins for the present" (2006 139). "In contrast to *Saving Private Ryan*, this independent film [*Memento*] offers a critique of the national narrative, using character memory, a fragmented narrative structure and national allegory to deterritorialize the triumphal narrative that dominates many American action-images" (2006 121). Like Geoff King, Martin-Jones argues that form itself can be a means for challenging dominant ideologies and argues that *Memento*'s "jumbled" narrative can be seen as a coded attack on triumphalism. "*Memento* turns the trajectory of the rape-revenge narrative on its head, illustrating that such killings are tantamount to getting away with murder . . . *Memento* encourages identification with a character who is lying to himself, by creating a false origin to a rape-revenge narrative, in order to commit murder" (2006 142). The focus here is on the way in which *Memento* disrupts narrative expectations, and Martin-Jones's emphasis is on the way in which this disruption challenges not only Hollywood conventions, but the larger ideological framework in which those conventions have developed and been employed in the cinema throughout the twentieth century. In his account, trauma enables or becomes an excuse for a form of self-deception used by Leonard to hide the truth from himself. Spectators, in identifying with Leonard, become implicated in his self-deception and his criminality, much like America itself has become implicated in the horrors of Abu Ghraib and Guantanamo Bay.

This reading of *Memento* takes place in a book in which Martin-Jones argues that many films made in the U.S. must hide their critiques of the status quo in order to meet the demands of industry and audience. His interpretation of films like *Memento* and *Eternal Sunshine* maintains that they can be understood on (at least) two levels and his (often strained) interpretations are focused on their function as particularly American films and the way they negotiate issues of national identity. *Memento*, argues Martin-Jones, offers the knowing audience more than just an exciting roller-coaster ride of a film: it also exposes the way in which unjust violence is often justified in American cinema.[6] The dialectical tension generated by *Memento* raises not simply aesthetic but ideological matters for the perceptive spectator: in its exhibitionistic subversion of expectations, *Memento* offers a critique of the American national narrative of triumphalism as well as a critique of the way in which Hollywood often fosters nationalism through the use of the rape-revenge narrative. That is, the subversion of the rape-revenge scenario does not simply call attention to form, but also to the ideological underpinnings of the form itself. So, much like how McGowan views *Mulholland Drive*, Martin-Jones views *Memento* as a type of countercinema, offering a critique not only of American triumphalism but also of the way in which classical Hollywood cinema often supports this triumphalism. *Memento*, as a product of the New Hollywood, however, must make this critique subtly—so subtly, in fact, that it is easy to miss.[7]

Ruth Perlmutter, in her reading of *Memento*, focuses not so much on the way the film disrupts the conventions and ideologies of Hollywood cinema as on the way in which it is used to explore Leonard's attempt to hide from himself a reality he would rather not face. She argues that Leonard, like the characters who populate trance films, seeks to cope with the traumatic events of his past by seeking "a new identity to ward off either a guilty or grief-stricken past concerning his wife's murder" (2005: 129). His anterograde amnesia is a form of "self-erasure" that allows him to forget "what he thinks he remembers" (2005: 129). Amnesia is "a convenient psychic malady for those suffering a damaged identity, [since] to forget is often a necessary and merciful defense against confronting an unbearable event" (2005: 130). Perlmutter suggests that this has led to Leonard's struggle with solipsism: "All the multiple tools of discovery—photos, body tattoos, mirror images, reverse order sequences that are always in the present time—suggest that everything seen and heard not only destabilizes character logic and questions objective reality, but also may only be inside the character's head. As a reinforcement of this suggestion, the dialogue is peppered with sayings that reflect on the desire and need to know that the world exists outside the self" (2005: 130). Leonard, for example, makes the following statement near the end of the film: "I have to believe in the world outside my own mind. I still have to believe that my actions have meaning, even if I can't remember them. I have to believe that when my eyes are closed, the world's still there. But do I? Do I believe the world's still there? Is it still out there?" Leonard's choice to trust no one, combined with his own self-deception, has led him to a precarious situation in which he must believe the evidence of the unseen (the not-remembered). The result is not only that is Leonard a solipsist, but that the entire film, not just the lying flashbacks, might be some sort of subjective realist fantasy or solipsistic nightmare. Is Leonard, like Sammy Jankis, a patient in an asylum? Is he dreaming? Hallucinating? Is the entire film a figment of his imagination? If it were, it would place *Memento* alongside *Caligari*, narrated from the perspective of the institutionalized mental patient. *Memento* certainly has other things in common with *Caligari*, particularly its lying flashbacks and numerous unresolved narrative questions regarding the identity of the narrator, so the comparison does seem apt. Leonard's answer to the question of whether he believes the world is still out there, however, is yes, he does; and Perlmutter, accordingly, does not conclude that the film is solipsistic in this manner, she simply suggests it as a possibility. She is not alone, however, in raising the possibility that this belief, like many of Leonard's other beliefs, may not be justified, or true.[8]

Memento's narrative complexity is multifaceted. Not only does it use an entirely new temporal framework: the retrogressive analeptic, but it also includes narrative strands that are subjective realist and ultimately, unreliable. As we have seen, the unreliability results from the fact that Leonard is the source of much of the information provided to spectators, and an important result of this is that many of the sequences in the film that are initially taken to be flashbacks turn out to be fictional, that is, they are not memories but acts of Leonard's imagination. As his stories become questionable, so does the very basis of his actions in the film. This throws Leonard's character radically into question: if he is not who he says he is, who is he really? The questions posed by Leonard's stories in *Memento* contrast somewhat with the type of challenges posed by the ontological shifts of *Mulholland Drive*, where the transition from the dream sequence to the waking strand is not clearly marked. The difference between the two is that in Memento, the embedded narrative is clearly marked, first by Leonard's voice-over, and second, by the use of black-and-white cinematography. The *crucial* difference is that Memento's embedded narratives are presented as factual, as a representation of memories. This sets up expectations that are then subverted when it is revealed that they are actually fictions rather than memories.

In terms of my argument regarding multiform narrative, we can see the shifts to the lying flashbacks in Memento as ontological rather than temporal. Leonard has deceived himself to the point that he believes his stories are true, and the unsuspecting spectator mistakes fiction for fact. This is similar to the way in which spectators of Mulholland Drive may believe that movement one is truth rather than fantasy, and why they may have trouble accepting an oneiric reading. The multiple ontologies of Memento, though different in substance from those of Mulholland Drive (lying flashbacks versus dreams), serve a similar purpose: they represent Leonard's confusion (self-deception?) over what is real and what is not. Memento uses a subjective realist style of narration and a progressive-analeptic temporality that subverts the conventional, linear causal dimensions common in the cinema and this subversion creates epistemological difficulties for spectators that are similar to those experienced by Leonard himself. Further, the use of the rape-revenge plot, in conjunction with a narrational style that limits information almost exclusively to the subjective realist perspective of Leonard, places spectators in a position in which empathetic alignment with Leonard is nearly inescapable. This makes the revelation that his motivations are fabrications all the more powerful for spectators, who mistakenly assume the film will adhere to rape-revenge convention, and so get a shock when it does not.

As for the question of classification, Memento proves to be more challenging than Mulholland Drive. Stylistically, it clearly employs an experimental narrative of the kind common to the art cinema, and shares this with Mulholland Drive. It was financed and distributed primarily by Newmarket Films, and made on a very modest budget of (an estimated) five million dollars (IMDb). As such, Memento had by far the lowest budget of the films under consideration and was also, perhaps, the most independently produced as well. Memento is also a prime example of Sconce's smart film in terms of marketing and provides a clear example of the way in which contemporary cinema often employs complex narrative as an attraction. By using a highly complex narrative structure to confound and surprise spectators, its pleasures, though similar to the roller-coaster-like thrills of the blockbuster, are generated not via special effects or explosions, but narratively, in a subjective realist multiform structure with nonlinear plotting, lying flashbacks, and a surprising disruption of expectations. Consequently, Memento is an excellent example of both the low-budget cinema of attractions, and of the subjective realist multiform cinema. Analyzing Memento in this manner provides yet another demonstration of the usefulness of the subjective realist multiform as a category for making distinctions in the field of complex narratives.

Notes

1. Generically, Memento has strong affinities with film noir. This affinity, however, is evident more in relation to its characters, structure, and themes than its mise-en-scène. Memento's characters resemble stock noir types such as the *femme fatale* (Natalie), the shady cop (Teddy), and the hard-boiled detective (Leonard). It uses noir-inflected voice-over narration—both *confessional* (Leonard explains the process by which he has become a criminal); and *investigative* (he explains how he has solved the murder) (Turbett 2001: 6). Its use of flashbacks and complex temporality, and its theme of insurance fraud, as well as its central character's attempt to create a new identity for himself in an effort to escape grief and guilt, clearly demonstrate its debt to noir. These affinities, however, are far from simplistic, and Dion Turbett argues that Memento, rather than simply employing the conventions of noir straightforwardly, dismantles its stereotypes, leaving them standing "as signifiers that problematize identity rather than assure it" (2001: 6). Turbett adds, "types are another way in which Leonard's subjectivity encroaches on the film world" (2001: 7). In terms of studio-era Hollywood filmmaking, film noir was often a genre in which directors were able to experiment with narrative and the fact that Memento uses it as a generic point of departure is not surprising. Memento's complexity, however, does seem to push the boundaries.
2. Logically, it seems impossible that Leonard would have this suspicion, since he would not have been able to remember the phone call, or the note Teddy slips under the door immediately after. That is, unless Leonard has written notes that the spectator is not made aware of.
3. In my own experience, on a first viewing of the film, I simply refused to accept the possibility that Teddy's version of events might be true, and saw his murder as justified. This can be seen as evidence of how successfully the narrative positions spectators to identify with Leonard.
4. Since Memento, Gaspar Noe has pushed the form to nauseating new heights in *Irreversible* (2002).
5. Martin-Jones's *Deleuze, Cinema and National Identity* examines a group of international films with complex narratives (many of them multiform) through a Deleuzean framework in order to show how the films negotiate issues of national identity. He argues that these films generally use complex narrative forms to problematize national identity in a time of global upheaval. Martin-Jones's goal is to illustrate how "Deleuze's theories can broaden our understanding of the way national identity is constructed in cinema" (2006: 1). He includes these films in a larger body of films made from the mid 1990s, including *Too Many Ways To Be Number One*, Hong Kong, 1997; *Sliding Doors*, Britain, 1997; *Run Lola Run*, Germany, 1998; *Chaos*, Japan, 1999; and *Peppermint Candy*, Korea, 2000. He has chosen these films for the following reasons: "Firstly, they each share a common concern with the manipulation of narrative time . . . Secondly, they all use their unusual narratives to examine recent

transformations of national identities" (2006: 1). He argues that films with fragmented narratives often appear in "times of historical transformation" and that these films can be seen as an "expression of the difficulty of narrating national identity at a time of historical crisis or transformation" (2006: 1). He illustrates this through the example of European postwar cinema, which often expressed "modernity's confrontation with its own limitations as a defining metanarrative" (2006: 2). The fragmented forms of European art cinema were a way of expressing the problematization of both the "notion of enlightened historical progress" as well as "the dominance of the nation as a framework within which identity could be structured" (2007: 2). (Both of these can be seen as embodied in the narrative forms of the commercial cinema of the day.) Fellini's 8½ is contrasted with Capra's *It's A Wonderful Life* to illustrate. In Capra's film, a parallel world is introduced to show George Bailey (James Stewart) the world that would have existed if he were not born; however, this "temporary departure from a singular, linear view of time was used to reinforce the legitimacy of one true time, and indeed, to conflate this 'correct' view of time with the film's one true vision of postwar American national identity" (2006: 4). In Fellini's film, by contrast, the parallel worlds which Guido (Marcello Mastrianni) inhabited "expressed the seeming impossibility of finding one informing, linear national narrative at a time of historical transformation in Italy" (2006: 4). He refers to the different strategies of these two films as "reterritorialization" and "de-territorialization" of national identity. In Martin-Jones's interpretations, fragmented narratives are read as attempts to renegotiate national identity, but the example from *It's A Wonderful Life* demonstrates how in its more conservative forms (e.g., Hollywood), ontological fragmentation is temporary and ultimately subsumed, re-territorialized, re-asserted into "a linear narrative of national identity" (2006: 5). *It's A Wonderful Life* is an example of a movement-image (classical Hollywood narrative), whereas 8½ is an example of a time-image (art cinema narrative).

6. His argument also echoes Rushton's idea of an anti-theatrical cinema in which subversions of expectations create a dialectical tension between the spectator's desire for absorption and his or her awareness of cinematic illusion.

7. Martin-Jones's argument is based on Deleuze's contrast of the "movement-image" with the "time-image." The notion of the time-image grew out of Deleuze's analysis of European art cinema and is broadly based on the various new waves and their experimentations with fragmented narratives, whereas the movement-image is broadly based on films that use a classical Hollywood continuity style (Martin-Jones 2006: 8). The contemporary films Martin-Jones writes about problematize Deleuze's clear-cut distinctions, since they no longer fit the hybridized contemporary examples. Martin-Jones identifies the films he is dealing with not as "commercial pap" or the work of "an auteur's genius," but as "products aimed at specific markets" (2006: 8). This strategy avoids the sharp either/or of the movement-image versus time-image and resembles Sconce's use of smart cinema to situate similar films in relation to Hollywood and its new industrial modus operandi as well as showing "how once clearly demarcated styles of filmmaking are now blending together in an attempt to cross over into different markets" (2006: 8). And, in the first chapter, he argues that contemporary cinema's use of what Deleuze calls the time-image should not be taken as an indication that as a culture we have undergone a radical change in our conception of time. Martin-Jones writes:

> Rather, *these 'hybrid' movement-/time-image films are time-images, to a greater or lesser degree, 'caught in the act' of becoming movement-images*. In spite of the

increasing manipulation of narrative time in recent cinema, the reterritorialising strength of the movement-image ensures its continuing dominance . . . I conclude that the many hybrid films made since the mid 1990s and discussed in the following chapters use their unusual time schemes to negotiate transformations of national identity. Thus by contextualising Deleuze's work within the parameters of the nation I am able to critique the often universalizing conclusions that he draws from the interaction between the two images. (2006: 19)

In my view, this "caught in the act" idea is simply another way of saying that these films, regardless of how fragmented the narratives are, are not time-images in the Deleuzean sense since, in the end, they can be arranged to produce a coherent linear whole. This can be illustrated by comparing *Lost Highway* and *Mulholland Drive*. While both films might appear to be incoherent, poetic, or experimental films—Deleuzean time-images in other words—*Mulholland Drive*'s fragmentation is (or can be read as) ultimately being re-territorialized by the logic of the classical narrative/movement-image. It is a hybrid in a way *Lost Highway* is not. The problem with this sort of approach is similar to the problem I encountered in the Freudian readings of *Mulholland Drive* and this is simply that the interpretive framework very often seems to lead to poor or untenable interpretations of the films in question.

8. A case could be made for a solipsistic reading on the basis that, late in the film, there is what Bordwell describes as a "wipe-by cut metamorphosis" in which a shot of Sammy Jankis in an institute becomes a shot of Leonard (2006: 140). This metamorphosis suggests that Sammy may well be Leonard's alter ego.

Chapter 6

ETERNAL SUNSHINE OF THE SPOTLESS MIND

Of the three key films under consideration, *Eternal Sunshine of the Spotless Mind* is possibly the most difficult to classify. Produced by Universal's "specialty" film production company Focus Features, it was made on an estimated twenty million dollars, a budget four times that of *Memento*. Unlike *Mulholland Drive* or *Memento*, *Eternal Sunshine* features Hollywood stars (A-list veteran Jim Carrey and *Titanic*'s Kate Winslet) in leading roles, and in this sense, is more akin to what Schatz calls the A-class star vehicle than the independent feature (2004: 35).[1] In addition, *Eternal Sunshine* won an Academy Award in 2005 for Best Screenplay, and generically, its story follows a narrative arc similar to that of a romantic comedy, even if it does so in an unconventional manner. It is also the most commercially successful of the three key films and was seen by audiences far larger than those who saw *Mulholland Drive* and/or *Memento*. At the same time, *Eternal Sunshine* is clearly a smart film. Its target audience, although slightly broader than that of *Memento*, certainly includes the bespectacled, educated, bohemian audiences described by Sconce. Focus Features is not Universal Studios but its "independent" appendage.[2] Its subjective realist multiform narrative is innovative, surprising, and challenging. Aesthetically, it is indebted to surrealist cinema as well as early multiform films such as *Wild Strawberries*. So, *Eternal Sunshine* is both a conventional Hollywood genre movie *and* a subjective realist multiform film. It challenges the traditional categories used in film studies and becomes an example of the type of film for which the subjective realist multiform category proves most useful.

This chapter will explore the way in which *Eternal Sunshine* combines the conventions of Hollywood and those of art cinema to create a hybridized subjective realist multiform narrative. It will consider the ways in which a number of the narrative and aesthetic techniques of *Eternal Sunshine* are used to represent the subjective perspective of Joel as his memory is erased. It will also provide an analysis of the film's innovative use of sound bridges to exploit the multiple ontological structure of the narrative. In doing so, these sound bridges create examples of the narrative trope metalepsis—the crossing or defacing of diegetic boundaries in a fictional narrative by a voice or character from another level. (Metalepsis is to multiple ontologies what analepsis [flashback] and prolepsis [flash-forward] are to multiple temporalities.) By focusing on these sound bridges, I will show how they are used to link the multiple ontological levels of *Eternal Sunshine*'s multiform narrative.[3] Like the progressive-analeptic structure of *Memento*, sonic metalepsis can be seen as a novel aesthetic characteristic, one of the many examples of innovation emerging from contemporary multiform cinema. Considering it an instance of the subjective realist multiform cinema contextualizes *Eternal Sunshine*'s complexity and innovation in a tradition to which it clearly belongs without overlooking its industrial and generic links to mainstream Hollywood.

Eternal Sunshine tells the story of Joel Barish (Jim Carrey), whose girlfriend of two years, Clementine Kryzinsky (Kate Winslet), has recently walked out on him. When Joel attempts to make amends, Clementine does not recognize him, and he learns through a mutual friend that Clementine has had her memory erased by a new technology developed by a Dr. Howard Mierzwiak (Tom Wilkerson) of Lacuna Inc. Joel, who is devastated, visits Mierzwiak and decides to undertake the procedure as well. Almost immediately after erasing his memory, however, Joel meets Clementine as if for the first time, and the two begin again. Generically, *Eternal Sunshine* was marketed as a dramatic romance and has been described as a "date movie," an "inter-cranial action/romance," and even as a science fiction film.[4] *Eternal Sunshine* can also be seen as a star vehicle for Jim Carrey and as an auteur film, with Michel Gondry and Charlie Kaufman vying for authorship. When the formal characteristics of *Eternal Sunshine* are considered, the tension generated by its classic Hollywood/art cinema hybridity becomes apparent. So, although the story it tells operates within the constraints of the classical three-act narrative—much like writer Charlie Kaufman's earlier film *Adaptation,* which parodies the form while still employing it—*Eternal Sunshine* also includes marked departures from classical Hollywood–style narratives. Its boy-meets-girl, boy-loses-girl, boy-gets-girl story is told using a number of challenging aesthetic techniques including an anachronic temporality, radical spatial disruptions, and causal indeterminacy. In addition, it employs a unique visual language for representing memory and clearly foregrounds its own constructedness through stylistic and formal excesses. And, although *Eternal Sunshine* employs numerous special effects, many of these are produced via simple, low-budget, in-camera effects and nonlinear editing, rather than more expensive Computer Generated Imagery. In addition to the importance of the surrealistic spaces these effects produce, it is also important that they were created with a modest amount of money. Although *Eternal Sunshine* had a large budget compared to *Memento*, its twenty million dollars was still well below the average of a Hollywood film at the time, estimated at around seventy million dollars (IMDb).

The Philosophy of *Eternal Sunshine*

Unlike *Mulholland Drive* and *Memento*, which have both been the subject of numerous academic articles, surprisingly little has been published on *Eternal Sunshine*. However, the attention it has garnered is an indication that, unlike your average romantic comedy, *Eternal Sunshine* is taken seriously by at least some members of the academy. Philosophers, for instance, have shown interest in the film for what is seen as its position on the ethics of memory removal and its interpretation of the Nietzschean eternal recurrence, while several other scholars have offered neurological and/or psychological analysis of the film's representation of memory—which is generally considered accurate.[5] What I would like to do here is present a brief overview of some this work, particularly of that which is relevant to my own argument. Christopher Grau, for instance, is an academic philosopher who offers a reading of what he sees as *Eternal Sunshine*'s philosophy. The position *Eternal Sunshine* offers is situated by Grau in a long-standing philosophical debate on the ethics of memory removal. It is centered on the question of whether or not one should be allowed to erase traumatic memories if, in fact, it could be done safely and effectively. In order to demonstrate that this debate has particular relevance for our times (and not simply in relation to the fictional world of *Eternal Sunshine*), Grau cites a section from "The President's Council Report on Biotechnology" (1997) that makes recommendations on research into "memory-diminishing drugs," and how they might be used in the treatment of posttraumatic stress disorder.[6] After a summary of the philosophical debate and an analysis of what Grau sees as the film's position within it—which is the rather banal assertion that *Eternal Sunshine* offers an argument against the use of technology to erase memory—Grau concludes with the following: "*Eternal Sunshine* is, among other things, a valuable philosophical resource because it . . . shows us that the harm caused by voluntary memory removal cannot be satisfactorily understood solely in terms of harms that are consciously experienced" (2006: 128). For my purposes here, it is enough to show that, first, the issue of memory erasure as it appears in the film is less science fiction than it may seem, and second, that writers such as Grau have seen the film as implicitly offering a position on a long-standing philosophical debate on the matter.

In a related article, and in a similar manner, David Smith also considers the importance of the film's position on memory removal. Smith, however, uses a very different framework for analyzing its position. He argues that *Eternal Sunshine* explicitly rejects memory erasure on the basis that it offers its characters a faulty notion of "self-transcendence." The self-transcendence proposed in *Eternal Sunshine* is, of course, achieved via the procedure made possible by Mierzwiak, who explicitly offers the promise that by editing people's memories, he can change their lives for the better. Smith builds his case through an exploration of Nietzsche's concept of the "eternal recurrence," which he argues plays a central role in the story. He also notes that each of Kaufman's previous films features a critique of the transformative notions thought by their characters to be the means of change and self-discovery, and that Kaufman's acquaintance with the work of Nietzsche—who is mentioned in every film Kaufman has written—might well have informed the writing of the script. Smith cites *Thus Spoke Zarathustra* to demonstrate the validity of his claim: "Have you ever said Yes to a single joy? O my friends, then you have said Yes to *all* woe. All things are entangled, ensnared, enamored; if ever you wanted one thing twice, if ever you said 'You please me happiness! Abide, moment!' Then you wanted all back. All anew, all eternally, all entangled, all ensnared, enamored" (Smith 2005: n.p.). Smith argues that Joel has a realization during the erasure of his memories that has direct parallels to this idea of the eternal recurrence. What he realizes is that to say Yes to the joy he has experienced in his relationship with Clementine necessarily requires saying Yes to the pain as well. And, although Joel first asks Mierzwiak to leave him just one happy memory, he eventually decides he wants to call the erasure off altogether in order to retain the good memories, even though it means retaining the bad as well. *Eternal Sunshine*, argues Smith, is an exploration of an essential aspect of Nietzsche's philosophy, and, in the end, presents the notion that the transcendence sought by its characters can be achieved not through the denial of the past or in any attempt to erase it, but through its acceptance, and an acceptance of the fate that this entails. Smith uses the concluding scene of the film—in which Joel and Clementine, with the full knowledge of their previous failed relationship, decide to try again—to illustrate his point. He sees this conclusion as a hedged version of Nietzsche's Dionysian "Eternal Yes," an acceptance of fate and all of its vicissitudes. Like Grau, Smith reads the film as advancing a philosophical position that rejects the use of technology as a means of erasing traumatic memories, even if it can be done safely (e.g., with only minor brain damage, "on par, say, with a night of heavy drinking," as Mierzwiak puts it).

The work of academic philosophers such as Grau and Smith demonstrates that, like *Mulholland Drive* and *Memento*, *Eternal Sunshine* is considered important by scholars for more than just its amusing and cleverly narrated love story. Their use of the film to illustrate philosophical arguments is similar to the way in which writers like Hudson and Perlmutter have used *Mulholland Drive* or the way in which Martin-Jones uses *Memento*. Similarly, it also resembles the way in which European art cinema of the 1960s was often seen to illustrate the finer points of Kierkegaardian or Sartrean Existentialism. In short, it is accorded a similar status to that of an art film, and allowed to critically comment on the status quo in ways mainstream films generally are not. This, more than anything in particular these writers offer in terms of analysis, is what is central to their inclusion here. I would now like to move on to an analysis of the aesthetic and narrative structures of *Eternal Sunshine*, focusing on its three distinct movements.

I will analyze each of these three movements separately, exploring the multiform narrational strategy of the film, as well as its unconventional temporal, spatial, and causal dimensions. *Eternal Sunshine*'s ontological shifts will be considered, as will its subjective realism, in order to demonstrate its relationship to *Mulholland Drive* and *Memento*. In addition, I will focus on the many ways in which the narrative of *Eternal Sunshine* both conforms to and disrupts the conventions of Hollywood cinema.

Temporal Inversions

Movement one of *Eternal Sunshine* introduces Joel Barish and spans a forty-eight-hour period beginning the morning of Valentine's Day, 2004—when Joel meets Clementine on a commuter train on Long Island. It serves as the rather conventional first act of the film, in which the central characters are introduced, their key traits established, the status quo is defined, and then the status quo is disrupted. Joel is portrayed as a lonely introvert who is desperate for a relationship. He meets Clementine, an unstable but attractive extrovert, and the two are drawn together. Then, after what seems to be the beginning of a happy story, Joel sits in his car weeping after what spectators assume is a flash-forward.

Movement one is conventional in its narration, editing, and temporal regimes, which are in keeping with the continuity style. Several important narrative questions are posed in this first movement, and these are the direct result of the unconventional plotting of the film. One of these, already introduced above, is: What happened to cause the failure of the relationship? There are other questions raised in earlier scenes, as well; for instance, when Joel, rather than going to work, impulsively catches a train that takes him to a wintry beach at the far end of Long Island where he first encounters Clementine. During this sequence, spectators are informed, via voice-over, that Joel is not an impulsive person. The contrast between his actions and his self-confessed personality traits introduces the question of why he has ditched work and gone to the beach instead, then. Why is he acting contrary to the traits that define him as a causal agent? Other questions are raised as well, including what happened to his car and to the missing pages in his journal. Of course, spectators eventually learn the answers to these questions, as well as that his meeting Clementine, which appears to be by chance, is not. Neither is this the first time they have met. None of this information comes until much later in the film, however, because the fragmented temporal narration inverts cause and effect.

Joel's unplanned trip to Montauk, for instance, is shown before its cause—Clementine's suggestion that he meet her there.[7] Yet another matter that is unexplainable until later in the film takes place the morning after Joel and Clementine's first night out together. As Joel waits in the car for Clementine to retrieve her toothbrush, he is questioned by a boyish character, Patrick (Elijah Wood), as to what he is doing at Clementine's house. Patrick seems to know Joel and is obviously puzzled by his presence, where, by contrast, Joel (as well as the spectator) does not have the faintest idea who Patrick is. This scene adds to the set of unanswered questions posed in movement one that now include: Why did Joel skip work and go to a frozen beach if he is not impulsive? Who is Patrick and why is *he* at Clementine's house; and, how is it that he knows Joel if Joel does not know him? These questions and their subsequent answers illustrate that, although the first movement is temporally conventional, the film as a whole is not. It employs an anachronic structure that departs from "the 'first' temporality of the narrative" via a flashback and remains in this (flashback) temporality for the majority of the film (Cameron 2006: 65). Although anachronic narratives traditionally create a hierarchy in which the first temporality is primary and others subordinate (for the sake of coherence), many recent films like *Eternal Sunshine* modify the "classical flashback structure so that the traditional hierarchy of narrative temporality is undermined" (Cameron 2006: 65).

Eternal Sunshine's opening sequence is followed by an extended flashback that represents the events of the evening prior to it. The flashback, however, becomes the primary level of the narrative in the film and this has two important effects. First, as already mentioned, it inverts the causal relationships between many of the events in the film, and, next, it undermines the traditional hierarchy of narrative temporality. The cause of Joel's impulsiveness as well as of Patrick's inquisitiveness are explained by events which take place in movement two and which temporally precede movement one. Neither is clear, however, until the film returns to its initial temporality in its closing scenes. A further complexity is generated by the fact that embedded in the extended flashback that makes up the second movement is a narrative that represents another flashback. This flashback-within-a-flashback is *Eternal Sunshine*'s subjective realist strand and, like *Memento*, it uses a progressive analeptic temporality to recount events of the previous two years.

Movement two, then, begins with what seems to be a simple ellipsis, although it is actually an unmarked flashback. The fact that it is unmarked leaves spectators with the false impression of linear progression and leads to false inferences. So, after movement one presents an account of Joel meeting Clementine and their first date, the narration shifts to Joel sitting in his car outside Clementine's house, weeping. The temporal gap, as mentioned, raises questions for spectators such as what has caused the failure of this relationship that seems to have started so well? But also: Why have these details been passed over? The assumption that the film has flashed-forward, skipping to the end of the love affair, however, is mistaken, and the ellipsis that seems to have moved the narration forward has actually gone back, taking spectators to the day before the action of the first movement. That movement two is a flashback means that the meeting of Joel and Clementine in the first movement is not their first meeting at all but the beginning of their second romance, which can only take place after both of them have erased the memories of their previous relationship. The unmarked flashback sets up a false linearity in the transition from movement one to movement two, which is not revealed as such until the outset of movement three, where the narrative circles back in time to the end of movement one, where Joel sits waiting outside Clementine's house after their trip to the Charles River.

The anachronic temporality of *Eternal Sunshine* is a key characteristic of its narrative structure, and although it is not evident to spectators until nearly the end of the film, it is of crucial importance from the outset. Although a coherent understanding of the way this structure works is possible on an initial viewing of the film, rewatching almost invariably rewards the spectator with further insight. The complexity of the film's temporality is compounded by the retrogressive flashbacks of the embedded subjective realist strand of movement two, which presents the memory-erasure procedure Joel undergoes in reverse chronological order.

Subjective Realism

Eternal Sunshine's temporality is clearly unconventional. Its unmarked flashback is confusing, and its flashback-within-a-flashback even more so initially. When coupled with the spatial disruptions of the subjective realist strand, and the unmarked (or unclearly marked) ontological shifts, *Eternal Sunshine* seems to embody an attempt to employ every known method of disrupting temporality. One of the results of the complicated temporality of the film is that spectators are forced to pay attention to time in ways not common in more conventional cinema. As in *Memento*, temporality is foregrounded and becomes one of the many different forms of defamiliarization employed in its highly exhibitionistic display, and it is in the film's second movement when these strategies come to the fore.

Movement two is by far the longest of the three main segments of the film, and although the majority of its action centers on Joel's apartment the night he has his memory erased, it also includes several subplots centered around the Lacuna staff: Stan (Mark Ruffalo), Patrick, Dr. Mierzwiak, and Mary. One of these involves Clementine, as Patrick has recently stolen Joel's journal from the Lacuna offices and is using it an attempt to seduce her. In fact, it is through conversations between Stan and Patrick regarding this theft that the unconscious Joel is able to put together important pieces of the puzzle unfolding on the subjective realist strand (where he is reliving memories of his relationship with Clementine as they are being erased). At the beginning of movement two, Joel has learned that Clementine has erased her memory of their relationship. He has, as a result, decided to erase his memory as well, and in the opening scene, he is on his way home to undergo the procedure. (Spectators, who assume the scene is a flash-forward, are not informed of any of this.) After the scene outside Clementine's house, Joel is shown going home, answering his oafish neighbor Frank's (Thomas Jay Ryan) questions about his Valentine's Day plans with Clementine, taking a sedative, and then collapsing just before the Lacuna technicians arrive to begin the memory erasure. From the point of his collapse, there are two levels of narration in movement two: a waking strand and a subjective realist strand. The waking strand is set in the familiar world established in movement one, but in flashback mode (unmarked). The internal subjective strand, by contrast, is set in the mind of Joel and represents the memories of his relationship with Clementine prior to their erasure. It is a flashback-within-a-flashback and presents numerous events that have transpired in Joel's relationship with Clementine over the past two years. That what is seen is actually taking place in Joel's mind is not immediately evident to the spectator, since the shift to the subjective realist strand is not clearly marked.

Movement two is characterized, then, by continually crosscutting between the waking strand—where Joel is unconscious on his bed—and the subjective realist strand, where he is viewing/experiencing/reliving his memories. As this latter strand represents Joel's memories, it has a different ontological status from that of the waking strand, as well as a different set of rules regarding space, time, and causality. Once the shift to the subjective realist strand takes place, the type of continuity established in movement one slowly begins to give way and the first indication of the shift takes place just after the Lacuna technicians enter Joel's house to begin the erasure.

During this scene, Joel is shown lying in his bed while the earlier scene in which he talks to his neighbor Frank replays in the background. In this second, subjective realist instance of the scene with Frank, there are several visual and sonic disruptions that set it apart from earlier scenes and mark it as ontologically distinct: first, Frank is visible but out of focus; second, the dialogue—which is repeated verbatim from the earlier scene—is distorted and accompanied by electronic noise (possibly diegetic, generated by the electronic devices used in the erasure) as well as by a nondiegetic musical motif that is used in these early scenes of movement two.[8] The subjective realist strand features a retrogressive analeptic temporality—like that of the main strand of *Memento*—which begins with Joel's most recent memories and proceeds backward (a fact later explained by Mierzwiak). Each subjective realist scene represents a memory of an event that took place earlier. It follows then that Joel's memory of the discussion with Frank would be the first to be erased, since indeed it is the most recent.[9] The scene with Frank is the first instance of the subjective realist strand and the first of the film's numerous departures from the stable, coherent space of movements one and three.

The following scene is one in which Joel discovers that Clementine has had her memory of their relationship erased, and like the previous one, it contains numerous spatial and temporal disruptions. In the first, Joel is shown telling his friends Rob and Carrie (David Cross and Jane Adams) of his attempt to make amends with Clementine after the argument that has led to their breakup. As Joel tells the story—in which he buys Clementine a gift, takes it to her at work, finds that not only does she not recognize him, but that she has also obviously begun a relationship with Patrick—the narration shifts to a visual representation of the events he is narrating. Upon Joel's discovery of Clementine and Patrick kissing in Barnes and Noble, his departure from the bookstore is visually accompanied by a series of in-camera special effects that suggest the alternate ontological nature of the narration. First, as he departs, the bookstore is progressively plunged into darkness behind him. This effect conveys his devastation at both Clementine's lack of recognition and the kiss she shares with Patrick. It also indicates a departure from the stable space established in movement one for the more expressionistic space of the subjective realist strand of two, where the mise-en-scène reflects Joel's emotional state.

The second effect, which is a part of the same shot, occurs as Joel departs from the darkened bookstore. As he exits, the door takes him directly from the bookstore into the home of Rob and Carrie, where the scene began, and where he now finishes recounting his story. This is yet another very simple in-camera special effect, created by the use of a studio set in which these two different locations share a wall; the same door acts (impossibly) as both the exit of the bookstore and the entrance into Rob and Carrie's living room. Simple as it is, the effect creates a problem for the spectator, who, although by this point in the narrative may have begun to suspect some type of ontological shift has taken place, has not been provided with a clear explanation of the nature of this shift. Consequently, these disruptions remain unexplainable on a first viewing of the film. The effect these events produce on spectators, then, is not unlike those described by Todorov in his account of the fantastic and lead to the question: How can these seemingly unexplainable events be accounted for? (Another dimension of these disruptions is the way in which they foreground the fictional dimension of the story. The scenes that spectators are viewing have clearly been filmed in a studio in which the bookstore set shares a wall with the set of Rob and Carrie's living room. This type of exhibitionism is eschewed in the continuity style since it is understood to disrupt absorption in the narrative.)

The third and final disruption in this scene is a minor one and occurs when Joel concludes his story with the question: "Why would she do this to me?" Rob provides an answer by showing Joel a letter from Lacuna explaining that Clementine has had her memory of him erased, and that, further, she requests that his name never be mentioned to her again. As Joel looks at the letter, Clementine's name disappears from it. This acts as yet another clue that these scenes are representing the erasure of Clementine from Joel's memory. In Todorovian terms, the spectator (who has not already realized that there is a subjective realist strand in which the laws of the natural do not apply) will experience a hesitation in regard to how to understand these events. The hesitation does not last long in *Eternal*

Sunshine because, shortly after the scene at Rob and Carrie's house, it is made clear that what Joel is experiencing is actually taking place in his head. The cumulative effect of these three disruptions, however, is the undermining of the conventional realist style that has been employed in the film so far, and, although the disruptions begin subtly, they become progressively more pronounced as the subjective realist strand moves deeper into the past.

Immediately after the scene in which Rob reveals that Clementine has erased her memory, Joel visits the Lacuna offices three separate times. In the first visit, he learns about the memory-erasure procedure from Dr. Mierzwiak. In the second, he demands to have his memory erased. And in the third, a map of his memories is produced by Stan so that they can be erased that evening. During this third visit to Lacuna, Joel experiences an epiphany: he realizes he is actually unconscious and that what he is experiencing is in his mind as his memories are being erased. This realization is represented through a series of crosscuts between the waking and subjective realist stands and begins as he sits in the brain-mapping lab responding to a series of mementos he has brought to facilitate the mapping. During the procedure, there is a cut to the waking strand where Joel is shown, for the first time, lying unconscious in his bed with the memory-erasing apparatus strapped to his head. The shot of Joel tracks to a shot of Stan and Patrick, who are shown with their low-tech memory-erasing equipment, which seems to be malfunctioning. While Stan and Patrick discuss the technical problem, there is a cut back to the subjective realist strand, where Joel is still at Lacuna, now in Dr. Mierzwiak's office. The sound of Stan and Patrick's conversation, however, has carried across this cut into the subjective realist strand, and Joel—who is now aware of the conversation—looks around in bewilderment and searches for its source. He then leaves the room and enters the brain-mapping lab, where he finds Mierzwiak, Stan, and his doppelgänger, who is sitting in the chair where Joel sat in the previous scene. Joel is surprised at seeing himself and it is at this point that he realizes what is taking place. As he looks at his doppelgänger, he says to Mierzwiak: "You're in my head already aren't you?" To which Mierzwiak answers, "Yes, I suppose so. I suppose this is what it would look like." If the cause of the spatial and temporal disruptions have been ambiguous for the spectator up to this scene, they are no longer. The flashbacks are clearly taking place in Joel's head as the Lacuna technicians erase his memory. For spectators, this is the point where the fantastic becomes the fantastic uncanny, since the events can now be explained by natural laws: these events are possible since they are occurring in Joel's mind. (That the seemingly supernatural events are the result of a technological intervention is also the reason *Eternal Sunshine* has been considered a science fiction film.) Joel's own awareness of his situation is brought about, in part, by the fact that even though he is unconscious, he can hear Stan and Patrick's interactions—which are taking place in the waking strand of the narrative. In fact, one of the more interesting editing devices in movement two is its novel use of sound bridges at the transitions between the waking and subjective realist strands.

Sonic Metalepsis

Sound bridges, as they are normally used, provide continuity across shots separated by time and/or space. In *Eternal Sunshine*, however, sound bridges are used not only to link scenes with distinct spatiotemporal frames, but also those with distinct ontologies. More importantly, these sound bridges are often used in a manner that disrupts the boundaries between the narrative strands and in some cases, actually brings about their erasure. *Metalepsis* is the narratological term used by Gerard Genette to describe the crossing or effacement of boundaries that separate diegetic levels in a fictional narrative (1980: 236); *metaleptic sound bridge* is the phrase I will employ to refer to the sonic border crossings that occur in *Eternal Sunshine*. In order to describe these, I want to shift the linguistic metaphor for discussing the film's multiple narrative form from *strands*, a term which suggests narrative interweaving, to *diegetic levels*, which communicates the hierarchal nature of the relationship between the strands. According to Genette, all fictional narratives have two basic levels, an *extradiegetic* and an *intradiegetic*. The extradiegetic is the level at which the narration happens, and in film is represented by the camera-narrator; the intradiegetic is the primary level at which the story is being told and is one level up in the narrative hierarchy from the extradiegetic. Higher levels, referred to as *metadiegetic levels*, result if and when additional (embedded) narratives are generated within the diegetic world; thus, *Arabian Nights*'s stories-within-a-story and *Hamlet*'s play-within-a-play are examples of metadiegetic levels of narration. In cinema, metadiegetic levels can result from a number of different strategies, including but not limited to the representation of character memories, dreams, and/or hallucinations. In the case of *Eternal Sunshine*, the subjective realist narrative that represents Joel's memory is a metadiegetic level of narration, whereas the waking strand is the film's intradiegetic level.

The boundaries that separate the diegetic levels of a narrative differ depending on the relationship among the levels and can be either *illocutionary* or *ontological* (Ryan 2004: 439). If a metadiegetic narrative has the same ontological status as the intradiegetic, for example—as in the case of a flashback—the boundary that separates it from the intradiegetic level is *illocutionary*. Illocutionary boundaries, then, separate diegetic levels that are temporally and/or spatially distinct but ontologically similar. If, however, a metadiegetic narrative is fictional, or in some other way ontologically distinct from the intradiegetic—as in dreams, hallucinations, and lying flashbacks, for example—the boundary that separates it from the intradiegetic level is *ontological*. In *Eternal Sunshine*, the subjective realist strand of the narrative is separated from the waking strand by an ontological boundary, as it represents a distinct or alternate reality. Its subjective realist strand is not simply made up of memory sequences but involves acts of imagination that require agency on the part of Joel (e.g., when he takes Clementine "off the map" into realms of memory where she was not originally present).

In the majority of feature films with metadiegetic levels, the boundaries that separate the levels are rigid, and shifts in narration from one level to another are clearly marked. In the *Wizard of Oz*, for example, Dorothy's dream—which is metadiegetic—is presented in Technicolor, while the intradiegetic narrative appears in black and white. The shift is marked by the shift in color, and the boundary between the real and the oneiric is firm. Clearly marking diegetic shifts in this manner is one of the many conventions employed in the classical style to maintain narrative coherence. By contrast, the shifts in *Eternal Sunshine*, and in multiform films like 8½, are not always marked, nor are the ontological boundaries that separate diegetic levels always rigid. In fact, at least some of the complexity of multiform cinema is the direct result of these types of unmarked shifts between intradiegetic and metadiegetic levels of narration, as we have seen in chapters 4 and 5. In *Eternal Sunshine*, there are several shifts between the waking and the subjective realist levels that are unmarked. Some of these unmarked shifts are accompanied by sonic breaches of the ontological boundary as well, which has the effect of bringing this boundary into focus, and in some cases, causing its dissolution. Metalepsis is the term used to describe the effacement of the boundaries that separate diegetic levels in a fictional narrative, and there are two types: rhetorical and ontological (Ryan 2004: 441). An authorial intrusion, for example, is a form of rhetorical metalepsis. When Alfred Hitchcock speaks directly to the spectator at the beginning of *The Wrong Man* (1956), he temporarily disrupts the imaginary world of the film with a real-world, nondiegetic narration. Marie-Laure Ryan writes that rhetorical metalepsis is the interruption of a current narrative level by "a voice that originates in or addresses a lower level" (2004: 441). The boundary crossing of rhetorical metalepsis, as the name suggests, is verbal: it is the voice of a narrator or character that crosses from one diegetic level to another. Another example can be found in *Stranger than Fiction* (Marc Forster 2006), where a metaleptic voice-over is used to represent the narration of a novelist as she writes the story of the film's central character. The sustained use of metalepsis in the film is an exception to the rule, however, as instances of rhetorical metalepsis in the cinema are generally brief and leave the narrative boundary intact, even if more visible.

Ontological metalepsis, on the other hand, is a more destructive transgression of the boundaries that separate diegetic levels and actually results in the "bleeding together" of two or more levels (Eggington 2001: 213). An example can be seen in Hideo Nakata's *Ringu* (1998), where a character from a film-within-the-film, Sadako, crawls out of a television screen and into the home of the character Ryuji. In this scene, a character from a metadiegetic narrative (the film-within-the-film) enters the intradiegetic narrative, crossing the boundary between the levels, thus erasing the distinction between the two. As such, it is an example of ontological metalepsis, where it is a corporeal being (rather than just a voice) that crosses the diegetic boundary, causing the previously distinct levels of the film to bleed together. *Eternal Sunshine* features metaleptic boundary crossings of both the rhetorical and ontological types, and I would like to move now to examples of each, focusing particularly on the way sound bridges are used in the process.

The first instance of rhetorical metalepsis in *Eternal Sunshine* takes place only after a series of conventional sound bridges has been used to link scenes on the metadiegetic level (the subjective realist strand) with scenes on the intradiegetic level (the waking strand). These conventional sound bridges accompany a series of visual transitions early in the scene that establishes that Joel is actually in two places at once: on the metadiegetic level, he is in the laboratory at the Lacuna offices responding to various mementos so that a map of his memories of Clementine can be made; on the intradiegetic level, he is unconscious in his bed while his memories are being erased. Although the metadiegetic scene represents Joel's *memory* of the brain mapping and not the event itself, this distinction has not yet been made clear to spectators, who have been led to assume the narration represents a single ontology (with a linear temporality). These assumptions are disrupted, however, when a cut to the intradiegetic level shows the unconscious Joel in his bed with the Lacuna technicians Stan and Patrick at his bedside erasing his memory. In terms of levels of narration, the sound bridges linking the edits from Joel in the mind-mapping lab to him in bed take place at the transition from the deep, internalized focalization of the subjective realist strand to the externalized focalization of the waking strand. These sound bridges function conventionally in that they serve to provide continuity across the shot transitions. However, there is an important shift in narration that takes place late in the scene, and this results in a shift in the nature of the sound bridges as well.

The shift in narration results from Joel's increasing awareness that something is not as it seems, that he is somehow both awake and not-awake at the same time. This awareness is brought about, in part, by sonic metalepsis: the conversation between Stan and Patrick crosses the boundary between the waking (intradiegetic) and the subjective realist (metadiegetic) levels. An early indicator of this sonic border crossing takes place when Stan discovers what he thinks is a problem with his equipment. He says: "Patrick, can you check the wires, I am getting some sort of read out on my own voice here." What Stan's read out indicates is that Joel, who seems to be unconscious, can actually hear Stan's voice. This creates a sonic feedback loop on Stan's computer and further, indicates that the sound bridge spectators have just heard (in which Stan asks Patrick to check the wires) is not simply a conventional sound bridge, but it also represents content from the intradiegetic level that is crossing over the boundary into the sonic space of the metadiegetic level. The difference between this sound bridge and the earlier ones, then, is that it represents not *only* a sonic device employed to provide continuity across shot transitions, but also the direct subjective aural experience of Joel, who is the source of the spectator's knowledge on the subjective realist level of narration. As such, it is an example of a rhetorical-metaleptic sound bridge, in which a voice originating in a lower level—in this case, a dialogue on the intradiegetic level—crosses the boundary to address a higher level, the metadiegetic.

Interestingly, Joel's ability to hear what is taking place on the intradiegetic level results in a further destabilization of the boundary between the two levels and produces what can be described as ontological metalepsis. Initially, the content of the metaleptic sound bridge, that is, Stan and Patrick's exchanges, is intermingled with aural (disembodied) memories of Clementine's voice (as well as that of Mierzwiak). Yet, as the scene progresses, and the sound from Stan and Patrick's conversation continues, Joel develops a greater awareness of what is taking place. He eventually realizes that what he is experiencing (on the metadiegetic level) is some kind of dreamlike state accompanying the erasure; he also comes to understand—as a result of Stan and Patrick's conversation (the content of the sound bridges)—that Patrick has stolen his journal from Lacuna and is using it to seduce Clementine. Joel's full awareness of these matters marks the transition into yet another phase of narration characterized by an ever-increasing number of spatial and temporal disruptions, in which his self-consciousness is represented visually through several doppelgänger scenes and sonically through echoes, feedback, and distortion. The visual and sonic doubling, as well as the increasing sense of agency Joel gains on the metadiegetic level, are the direct result of the metaleptic sound bridges.

Ontological metalepsis, as we have seen above, occurs when the boundaries separating ontologically distinct diegetic levels are erased and the two worlds "bleed" together (Eggington 2001: 209). This is what eventually happens when the content of the sound bridges actually begins to shape the events of the metadiegtic level, which becomes not simply a representation of Joel's memories, but the blurring of his memories together with the content of the conversation taking place between Stan and Patrick. This can be seen clearly in the scene in which Joel and Clementine are having Chinese food in his apartment. As they eat, Joel overhears and comments on the conversation between Stan and Patrick, which begins as a sound bridge and continues after the transition as a voice-over. Joel imagines saying to Clementine, "There is someone here, they stole your underwear." To which she responds with a puzzled look, since, unlike Joel, she cannot hear the conversation (she is, after all, simply a figment of his imagination). The metadiegetic level has, by this point, ceased to simply be a collection of singular memories that are progressively being erased and has become, at the very least, a place where Joel's memories are actively interwoven with the content of the conversation taking place on a different level of the narrative. This means that the sonic overlap is no longer simply rhetorical but ontological; it has erased the distinction between intradiegetic and metadiegetic, past and present, waking and sleeping. The intradiegetic level, where Patrick and Stan discuss the ethics of panty theft, has become part of the metadiegetic level, which has now become something other than simply memory. This blurring of the boundary separating what were, up to this point, ontologically distinct diegetic levels of the narrative is a clear example of ontological metalepsis, or "reality bleeding" in the film (Eggington 2001: 209). These metaleptic sound bridges are simply one of the many strategies used in the film to navigate the various levels, strands, and temporalities of its multiform narrative world. Interestingly, the shifts from the intradiegetic to the metadiegetic levels, rather than remaining unmarked as they do in a film such as 8½, become quite clearly marked in *Eternal Sunshine*. One of the results of this is the reduction of ambiguity. As the film progresses, all of the temporal, spatial, and causal gaps introduced in the early parts of the film are resolved, and the film ends by satisfying the types of expectations commonly brought by viewers to classical Hollywood cinema. The metaleptic sound bridges, which are initially used to puzzle both character and spectator in the film, eventually function to reduce narrative complexity.

An important consequence of Joel's self-awareness on the subjective realist level is that it radically changes his experience of the memory-erasure procedure. Rather than passively experiencing the memories in the moment before they are erased, he becomes much more actively engaged, exercising an agency within them that he has lacked before. The agency he experiences on the self-conscious subjective realist level of the film becomes increasingly important as the memory-erasure procedure moves further back in time to erase the memories of the early days of Joel and Clementine's relationship, which have little of the negativity and pain attached to them that the later memories do. In one of these early memories, Clementine says to him, in a moment of tenderness, "Joel, don't ever leave me." As she finishes, however, Clementine is literally dragged out of the shot by an unseen source representing Lacuna. Joel, as if praying, says, "Mierzwiak, let me keep this memory, just this one." In the next scene, Joel and Clementine lie together again on the frozen Charles River at a high point in their relationship. Joel says to her, "I could die right now. I am just . . . happy. I am exactly where I want to be. I have never experienced this before." As Joel finishes, however, Clementine is once again removed from the memory, and it is at this point that Joel experiences his Nietzschean epiphany: he decides he wants to keep all of his memories and stop the procedure altogether. He yells, "I want to call it off. Can anybody hear me? I want to call it off." As these early memories of their relationship continue to be erased, the hopelessness of Joel's desire becomes evident, and in the following shot, Stan and Mary are shown dancing on Joel's bed, stoned, drunk, and postcoital while the computer erasing his memory continues on "autopilot."

Joel, realizing his dilemma, tries several different methods to thwart the erasure and preserve his memories. First, he hides Clementine by simply running from the spotlight that has come to represent one of the mechanisms of erasure in the mise-en-scène of the subjective realist. When this fails, he has a discussion with Clementine about the erasure in which she suggests that he try to wake himself up. He pries his eyes open on the subjective realist level and succeeds in opening his eyes on the waking strand, but only briefly. Finally, Joel decides to take Clementine where she "does not belong," by hiding her in memories that will not be erased, memories where she was not originally present. This strategy proves to be the most effective of all of those he tries, and each of his attempts are represented via a radically disrupted space and time that visually conveys the radical ontological nature of the events they represent. In one of these scenes, for example, an adult Clementine saves the child Joel from a group of bullies who are forcing him to kill an injured bird with a hammer. Clementine then morphs from adult to child and the two play a game from their adult relationship together. The color palette of the scene resembles a faded photograph from the late sixties or early seventies, which corresponds to the time period in which the memory would have originally taken place.

In another scene, the adult Joel and Clementine are bathed together in a sink by Joel's mother; and in yet another, Joel transforms Clementine into Mrs. Hamlin, a friend of Joel's mother. In these latter two scenes, forced perspective is used to distort the physical space in order to make the adult Joel (and Clementine in the latter) appear to be the size of a child. The effects are humorous, and yet also successful in visually communicating Joel's attempts at smuggling Clementine into his childhood memories. As a result of Joel's efforts, the memory-erasure program eventually malfunctions and Joel goes "off the map." The inebriated (and idiotic) Stan, unable to locate these new memories, is forced to call Mierzwiak, who eventually finds where Joel has hidden Clementine and completes the erasure. Before the procedure ends, however, Joel realizes that there is no hope in saving Clementine and movement two ends with Joel saying goodbye to Clementine in the beach house at Montauk, where they first met. Before Joel leaves and Clementine is utterly erased, however, she whispers, "Meet me in Montauk." This suggests that Joel's uncharacteristic ditching of work to go to the beach in Montauk the next day may have its source here, in a memory that is erased by Mierzwiak.

Movement two provides spectators of *Eternal Sunshine* a host of unconventional narrative devices drawn straight from the art cinema of the twentieth century, as well as adding a few new inventions of its own. It disrupts conventions of time, space, and causality as well as employing a fragmented ontology to represent the subjective perspective of Joel as his memory is erased. It is a highly exhibitionistic strand that is complex, yet finally comprehensible in the larger context of the film.

The Marvelous Real

When Joel wakes up the morning after the erasure, it is clear that the narration has circled back to where it began. The opening sequence of the film is repeated. Joel is shown, as in movement one, waking up, discovering his damaged car, waiting for the train that he takes to Montauk, where he encounters Clementine on the beach. The shots are presented elliptically and eventually return spectators to the point where movement one ended—with Joel sitting in his car outside Clementine's house the morning after their trip to the frozen river. The entire narrative has, up to this point, then, recounted the events of Joel and Clementine's previous relationship, their breakup, their memory erasures, and has now returned to the early stages of their second relationship—which is where movement one ended so abruptly.

When Clementine returns to Joel's car, however, she has an envelope that she has received with her files from Lacuna, as well as a cassette tape recording of herself explaining to Mierzwiak her reasons for wanting to erase Joel. It includes a scathing, uncensored, and in-depth analysis of Joel's faults. They listen to this tape together, which is puzzling for them both, but utterly devastating to Joel, who thinks Clementine is "fucking with his head." Joel ejects her from the car and returns home only to find that he has also received a package that contains a cassette on which he explains to Mierzwiak the reasons he wants to erase Clementine. The tapes have been sent, along with letters of explanation, by Mary, who, upon the discovery of her past relationship with Mierzwiak, has stolen all of the Lacuna files and mailed them to the former patients to whom they belong. Joel is listening to his tape when Clementine arrives, shortly after he has left her on the street. In the final scene of *Eternal Sunshine*, Joel and Clementine, after a clear recognition that they have failed to make a relationship work in the past, decide they will try again anyway, and thus the romantic arc of the narrative is made complete. And *Eternal Sunshine*, in this sense, offers its audience a much more conventional conclusion than does either *Mulholland Drive* or *Memento*. Indeed, by the time the film reaches this conclusion, all of the temporal, spatial, and causal gaps introduced are explained; all of its enigmas are resolved; and the film ends by providing the type of satisfaction expected by viewers of classical Hollywood cinema.

Eternal Sunshine is both similar to and different from *Mulholland Drive* and *Memento*. It is similar in that its subjective realist strand represents its central character's experience of an abnormal state of consciousness. Its disruptions of time and space are, like those that occur in *Mulholland Drive* and *Memento*, designed to represent Joel's experience of this alternate state of consciousness in a way that positions spectators to share the experience. *Eternal Sunshine*, then, like these other films, employs a subjective realist multiform narrative in a manner that is consistent with the way the form has been used in the cinema since *Caligari*. It challenges the conventions of the continuity style in a self-conscious and exhibitionistic manner and offers its spectators novelty and surprises consistent with the cinema of attractions. Unlike these other films, however, *Eternal Sunshine*'s disruptions are ultimately and completely subsumed by the classical narrative conventions that govern the waking strand of the narrative, which bookends the film. This conventionality does not negate the novel and surprising dimensions of the film; it simply makes them more palatable to the film's target audience, which includes but is not limited to those of the smart cinema. *Eternal Sunshine* is clearly an example of the contemporary, low-budget cinema of attractions. It is a wildly exhibitionistic film that employs multiple narrative strands, multiple realities, and a subjective realist narration to generate its complex yet ultimately comprehensible multiform narrative.

Notes

1. At the time of *Mulholland Drive*'s production, Naomi Watts was not a star; the same can be said for *Memento*'s Guy Pearce.
2. The "independent" distinction is of great importance in this claim since otherwise the comparison would be to *The Matrix* and *A Beautiful Mind*, both of which were far more commercially successful than *Eternal Sunshine*.
3. This analysis of sound in the film is partially motivated by Michel Chion's book *Audio-Vision*, particularly where he writes, "We must continue to refine and fill in our typology of film sound. We must add new categories—not claiming thereby to exhaust all possibilities, but at least to enlarge the scope, to recognise, define, and develop new ideas" (1994: 75).
4. See Hampton 2004: 32; and Norris 2004a: 20.
5. See Richard Gray (2007).
6. Since his article was published, testing on at least one of these drugs, *propranolol*, has been undertaken by scientists at Harvard, and, in a recent news report from the *Telegraph* on this research, science writer Richard Gray includes numerous references to *Eternal Sunshine*.
7. The ontological status of Joel's agreement with Clementine is of course problematic. It takes place in a memory that is not actually a memory, and what is more, it is erased before Joel wakes up. This explains why he does not remember the arrangement but does not explain how Joel and Clementine both end up in Montauk. Is it supernatural, the result of some psychic communication between the two? Is it coincindence? Fate?
8. This is a piano theme accompanied by what resembles a cymbal being struck with a drumstick while simultaneously being held.
9. Though in terms of the overall narrative continuity it is problematic, since this memory would not have been mapped by Stan and so could not have been targeted for erasure.

Conclusion

I have proposed in these pages that films such as *Mulholland Drive*, *Memento*, and *Eternal Sunshine* can be understood as art cinema/Hollywood hybrids, focusing on the ways in which they employ aesthetic and narrative techniques developed in the art cinema of the twentieth century in the very different industrial and generic contexts of the American cinema. In this sense, earlier theoretical categories such as modernism, formalism, or even art cinema—though certainly relevant in analyzing the narrative and aesthetic forms of these films—do not seem to provide adequate frameworks for describing them given the contexts from which they have emerged or the audiences they have attracted. Recent scholarship on "complex narrative" has certainly done much to bridge the gap between older categories and the latest cycle of narrative experimentation, and this book should be taken as an attempt to contribute further to this impetus. Where "complex narrative" has become a useful catch-all category for films that depart in significant ways from the classical Hollywood style, I have proposed the multiform and the subjective realist multiform as subcategories of complex narrative. The films that I have analyzed have been drawn from a range of time periods and movements, but my primary case studies have come from the art cinema and American independent cinema; through these films I have sought to show how filmmakers from Weine to Gondry have contributed to the development of the subjective realist multiform cinema. The films explored were chosen because of their subjective realist ontologies and fragmented narratives, and as such were shown to have affinities with the avant-garde cinema of twentieth century, a link that is important to recognize.[1]

One unintended result of this connection is that the parallels between these subjective realist multiform films and several other styles of cinema have come into focus. On the one hand, multiform films are related to the blockbuster, a crucially important contemporary form of the cinema of attractions. Although the Hollywood-style spectacle featured in the blockbuster is different from the type of attractions used in multiform cinema, it is similar by virtue of its exhibitionism. The spectacle of the blockbuster is designed to amaze, surprise, shock, and/or awe its audiences (in much the same way that the early films of Lumière and Méliès did). And, it is in this way that the sometimes astonishing narrative complexity and stylistic techniques devised to represent characters' subjective experiences in subjective realist multiform cinema is related to the blockbuster. On the other hand, by virtue of their comparatively low budgets and narrative complexity, the subjective realist multiform films we have considered are related to films that employ spectacles such as real sex (*Romance*), unusual styles of animation such as rotoscoping (*Waking Life*; *A Scanner Darkly* [Richard Linklater 2006]), or dangerous and asinine stunts (*Jack-Ass* [Jeff Tremaine 2002]) to draw their audiences. These types of films offer novel, titillating, surprising, or even shocking events as forms of attraction, and, what is more, they are made on extremely modest budgets. I have referred to this style of filmmaking as the low-budget cinema of attractions and argued that *Mulholland Drive*, *Memento*, and *Eternal Sunshine* fit within it. Each was made on a budget well below the industry average and employs complex and at times shocking narrative styles. These films also sit in the bottom tier of Schatz's threefold division of New Hollywood productions (blockbuster, star vehicle, independent film) in that they were made or distributed by "independent" appendages of the studios. Further, they are more complex than the average Hollywood film and are targeted at a global, niche audience of young, educated, DVD-buying audiences. Therefore, they are examples of Jeffrey Sconce's smart cinema (made in the hopes that they might possibly cross over and reach audiences as large as films such as *Pulp Fiction* do).

Subjective realist multiform cinema is useful for two key reasons, then. First, it situates films such as *Mulholland Drive*, *Memento*, and *Eternal Sunshine* in a historical context rather than treating them as entirely new forms (however novel these films may be). Rather than constituting a new mode of representation, subjective realist multiform films should be seen as part of a trajectory that runs from the early cinema to the New Hollywood and encompasses films as diverse as *Caligari*, *Persona*, *The Matrix*, and even *Inception*.[2] It situates present examples in relation to those of the past and emphasizes continuity rather than disjunction (or novelty). There are, of course, novel aspects to these films: *Memento*'s temporality and *Eternal Sunshine*'s sound bridges are genuinely innovative and have pushed the boundaries of what has come before, creating new experiences for spectators, particularly the mass audiences these films have reached.[3] What is not new, however, is the basic narrative structure of these films, which can be found in films dating back to the early decades of the twentieth century. The second reason the subjective realist multiform narrative is useful is that it offers a way of making distinctions between complex narrative forms that are often unhelpfully grouped together: the multiform and the multi-strand. The narrative complexity of multi-strand films such as *Crash* or *Syriana* results from their multiple strands, while *21 Grams* and *Babel* combine multiple strands with fragmented temporalities. *Mulholland Drive*, *Memento*, and *Eternal Sunshine*, by contrast, feature multiple strands, fragmented temporalities, *and* multiple ontologies. I have argued that it is the latter that clearly differentiates them from the multi-strand.[4] This distinction is simple, yet highly productive.

Mulholland Drive, *Memento*, and *Eternal Sunshine*, while they share many structural similarities, are, of course, also quite distinct from one another. Apart from their very different styles and stories, each represents a different point on the spectrum of narrative complexity. They are presented in an order that is meant to reflect, in some way, the journey of the subjective realist multiform narrative from its origins in the avant-garde cinema to its use in a Jim Carrey star vehicle. *Mulholland Drive* presents the most significant challenges for spectators and, in this respect, is the least conventional and most distinct from the classical Hollywood style. The difference results from its ambiguous or unmarked ontological shifts and its lack of a clear, coherent story. (By contrast, consider *A Beautiful Mind*, which also employs a subjective realist mode of narration and unmarked ontological shifts but ultimately subsumes them within a much more coherent narrative without significant aporias.) The story *Mulholland Drive* tells cannot be definitively articulated, although, as we have seen, there are dramatically different understandings of the degree to which the film can be said to be coherent or otherwise. What seems beyond question, however, is that *Mulholland Drive* is not a film intended for a mass audience but rather for what Denby has described as a knowing audience. In this sense, it is a part of an older tradition of art cinema and is slightly different from smart films such as *Memento* and *Eternal Sunshine*.

Memento is undoubtedly the most innovative and novel of my key examples, yet it can also be seen to be more conventional in narrative terms than *Mulholland Drive*. Its complexity results from several strategies, the most important of these being its progressive analeptic temporality and lying flashbacks. Its temporality—which was unique at the time of the film's release—inverts cause and effect in a manner that challenges comprehension while not stifling it. The confusion it creates is designed to mimic the effects of Leonard's condition and forces spectators to learn a new set of rules. The lying flashbacks, on the other hand, create different challenges for the spectator, who is positioned to sympathize and identify with Leonard. When the mendacity of his "memory" is revealed late in the film, it comes as a shock to the spectator. Regardless of *Memento*'s complicated plotting, however, a largely coherent story can be assembled in the end (even if some important narrative questions do remain). This conservative understanding of *Memento* does not diminish its creative achievement; in fact, part of the genius of the film seems to be that it is highly complex *and* yet ultimately comprehensible. In this sense, *Memento* can be seen as a film that combines the narrative complexity of the art cinema with the comprehensibility and coherence of classical cinema, and so, it sits at the center of the spectrum of complexity I have used to compare these three films.

Eternal Sunshine is similarly recoupable in narrative terms. All of its fragments and enigmatic moments can be organized into a clear set of causal relations in space and time. Its narrative is organized around its central character, Joel, who has a clearly defined and consistent set of traits and whose journey from one disrupted status quo to a new state of equilibrium closely resembles the arc of the classical narrative. This explanation, while it may not adequately reflect the fragmented manner in which the events of the story are presented, does accurately summarize the story structure: Joel meets Clementine, loses her, then wins her back. In this way, the story of *Eternal Sunshine* looks similar to the stories of dozens of romantic comedies made by Hollywood. For fans of *Eternal Sunshine*, however, one of its many unique pleasures it offers is the challenge of assembling a coherent story out of the temporally, spatially, and ontologically fragmented plot. Of course, it is important that a coherent story *can* be assembled. In fact, on this point, it seems that a generalization can be made about the relationship between narrative incoherence and box office returns: the greater the degree of incoherence, the smaller the audience. A film can be complex, it can disrupt expectations, but it must finally make narrative sense if it is to attract large audiences. *Eternal Sunshine*, although conventional in regard to the story it tells, uses a complex narrative to tell it. It is innovative and exhibitionistic in terms of style and it reached a relatively wide audience while being produced on a very modest budget; it is, then, like *Mulholland Drive* and *Memento*, an example of what I have called in these pages the low-budget cinema of attractions. Like the high-profile multi-strand films *Crash* and *Babel*, multiform films such as *Eternal Sunshine* and *Memento* have unusually complex narratives, and yet have proven to be viable commercial properties; consequently, many other films like them have followed. *Eternal Sunshine*, made nearly a decade after *Pulp Fiction*, grossed over thirty-four million dollars at the U.S. box office—not as lucrative as *Pulp Fiction*, but still outstanding for an independently produced feature. (When one considers that domestic theatrical box-office earnings are merely the first step in a film's economic journey, these statistics become even more impressive.)

Interestingly, the release of *Inception* in 2010 seems to be both a part of the cycle as well as something different again. *Inception* is a complex film, featuring six distinctive ontological levels and using a complex regime of crosscutting and endless streams of exposition to ensure comprehensibility. It is the first subjective realist mutiform action blockbuster. Made on a budget of $160 million, it went on to make over $800 million at the box office. As such, *Inception* may well be the culmination of the cycle of complex narrative films begun by *Pulp Fiction*, but it almost certainly marks the beginning of something else altogether as well. With this in mind, I would like to return to *New Yorker* film critic David Denby's musing on this cycle, where in the midst of his insightful analysis, he poses the following: "Some of the directors [of these complex films] may be just playing with us or, perhaps, acting out their boredom with that Hollywood script-conference menace the conventional 'story arc.' But others may be trying to jolt us into a new understanding of art, or even a new understanding of life. In the past, mainstream audiences notoriously resisted being jolted. Are moviegoers bringing some new sensibility to these riddling movies?" (2007: n.p.). While it is certain that these films are made because they are commercially viable, I would argue that mainstream moviegoers *are* bringing a new sensibility to these complex films. They have discovered the pleasures of narrative complexity that were formerly reserved for art-house audiences and want more.[5] Their willingness to struggle through the disruptions and dislocations, to find pleasure in making sense of challenging narratives, and most importantly, to pay for the opportunity to do so will certainly result in the further exploitation of these forms. This book represents my own attempts to understand this cycle of films, as well as to contribute to the work of comprehending and analyzing the narrative styles they employ.

Notes

1. My choice of films has, of necessity, been limited, and most certainly could have been different given the numerous films with subjective realist multiform narratives made

in contexts other than those I have drawn from. Contemporary European and Asian cinema, as well as mainstream Hollywood, are all rich sources of examples, as a look at contemporary work on complex narrative indicates.
2. I have also argued that subjective realist multiform films are different from science fiction and fantasy films that use multiform narratives, however, since the alternative realities of these genres are technologically driven, futuristic, or fantastic in origin, rather than purely subjective.
3. They have also been much imitated. BBC TV's *Life On Mars* (2006–07), for instance, an art cinema–inspired cop show, features metaleptic sound bridges in every episode. In some respects, the series could be said to be built around these sound bridges, which link the hallucinatory primary strand with the (largely unseen) real world.
4. It is, however, their multiple strands that distinguish them from films such as *Fight Club*—which uses a subjective realist perspective without multiple diegesis.
5. That is, as long as the films are not too complex, feature recognizable stars, and do not challenge the status quo.

Filmography

Amores Perros. Dir. Alejandro González Iñárritu, 2000.
Arrival of a Train at La Ciotat Station. Dir. Auguste Lumière and Louis Lumière, 1895.
Avatar. Dir. James Cameron, 2009.
Babel. Dir. Alejandro González Iñárritu, 2007.
Back to the Future. Dir. Robert Zemeckis, 1985.
A Beautiful Mind. Dir. Ron Howard, 2001.
Being John Malkovich. Dir. Spike Jonze, 1999.
Black Ice. Dir. Stan Brakhage, 1994.
Blind Chance. Dir. Krzysztof Kieslowski, 1981.
Bottle Rocket. Dir. Wes Anderson, 1996.
Brainstorm. Dir. Douglas Trumball, 1983.
Brazil. Dir. Terry Gilliam, 1985.
Blow Up. Dir. Michelangelo Antonioni, 1966.
The Bride Retires. France, 1902.
The Cabinet of Dr. Caligari. Dir. Robert Weine, 1919.
Chaos. Dir. Hideo Nakata, 1999.
Un Chien Andalou. Dir. Luis Buñuel, 1927.
Citizen Kane. Dir. Orson Welles, 1941.
Crash. Dir. Paul Haggis, 2004.
Crossfire. Dir. Edward Dmytryk, 1947.
Dark City. Dir. Alex Proyas, 1998.
Die Hard. Dir. John McTiernan, 1988.
La Dolce Vita. Dir. Federico Fellini, 1960.
Donnie Darko. Dir. Richard Kelly, 2001.
Down by Law. Dir. Jim Jarmusch, 1986.
Easy Rider. Dir. Dennis Hopper, 1969.
8½. Dir. Federico Fellini, 1962.
The English Patient. Dir. Anthony Minghella, 1996.
Eternal Sunshine of the Spotless Mind. Dir. Michel Gondry, 2004.
Fight Club. Dir. David Fincher, 1999.
Fire Walk With Me. Dir. David Lynch, 1992.
The Fisher King. Dir. Terry Gilliam, 1991.
Flirt. Dir. Hal Hartley, 1995.
The Fountain. Dir. Darren Aronofsky, 2006.
The Game. Dir. David Fincher, 1997.
The Godfather. Dir. Francis Ford Coppola, 1972.
Golem. Dir. Paul Wegener, 1915.

Gosford Park. Dir. Robert Altman, 2001.
The Graduate. Dir. Mike Nichols, 1968.
Groundhog Day. Dir. Harold Ramis, 1993.
Gummo. Dir. Harmony Korine, 1997.
Happiness. Dir. Todd Solondz, 1997.
Hard Eight. Dir. P.T. Anderson, 1997.
How Green Was My Valley. Dir. John Ford, 1941.
Inception. Dir. Christopher Nolan, 2010.
Intimacy. Dir. Patrice Chereau, 2001.
Intolerance. Dir. D.W. Griffith, 1916.
Irreversible. Dir. Gaspar Noe, 2002.
It's a Wonderful Life. Dir. Frank Capra, 1946.
Jack-Ass. Dir. Jeff Tremaine, 2002.
Jaws. Dir. Steven Spielberg, 1975.
The Jazz Singer. Dir. Alan Crosland, 1927.
Julien Donkey-Boy. Dir. Harmony Korine, 1999.
The Lady in the Lake. Dir. Robert Montgomery, 1947.
Last Year at Marienbad. Dir. Alain Resnais, 1961.
Laura. Dir. Otto Preminger, 1944.
The Locket. Dir. John Brahm, 1946.
The Lord of the Rings. Dir. Peter Jackson, 2001.
Lost Highway. Dir. David Lynch, 1997.
Magnolia. Dir. P.T. Anderson, 1998.
A Man and a Woman. Dir. Claude Lelouch, 1966.
The Matrix. Dir. Andy Wachowski and Lana Wachowski, 1999.
Memento. Dir. Christopher Nolan, 2000.
Meshes of the Afternoon. Dir. Maya Deren, 1943.
Metropolis. Dir. Fritz Lang, 1927.
Mothlight. Dir. Stan Brakhage, 1963.
Mulholland Drive. Dir. David Lynch, 2001.
Mystery Train. Dir. Jim Jarmusch, 1989.
Nashville. Dir. Robert Altman, 1975.
A Nightmare on Elm Street. Dir. Wes Craven, 1984.
Night on Earth. Dir. Jim Jarmusch, 1991.
9 Songs. Dir. Michael Winterbottom, 2004.
Nosferatu. Dir. F.W. Murnau, 1922.
Paisa. Dir. Roberto Rossellini, 1946.
Peppermint Candy. Dir. Chang-Dong Lee, 1999.
Persona. Dir. Ingmar Bergman, 1966.
The Piano Teacher. Dir. Michael Haneke, 2001.
The Prestige. Dir. Christopher Nolan, 2006.
Psycho. Dir. Alfred Hitchcock, 1960.
Pulp Fiction. Dir. Quentin Tarantino, 1994.
Raiders of the Lost Ark. Dir. Steven Spielberg, 1981.
Rashomon. Dir. Akira Kurosawa, 1951.
Ringu. Dir. Hideo Nakata, 1998.
Romance. Dir. Catherine Breillat, 1999.
Run Lola Run. Dir. Tom Tykwer, 1998.
A Scanner Darkly. Dir. Richard Linklater, 2006.
Se7en. Dir. David Fincher, 1995.

sex, lies, and videotape. Dir. Steven Soderbergh, 1989.
Short Cuts. Dir. Robert Altman, 1993.
The Sixth Sense. Dir. M. Night Shyamalan, 1999.
Slacker. Dir. Richard Linklater, 1991.
Sliding Doors. Dir. Peter Howitt, 1998.
Sling Blade. Dir. Billy Bob Thornton, 1996.
Source Code. Dir. Duncan Jones, 2011.
Star Wars. Dir. George Lucas, 1977.
Strange Days. Dir. Kathryn Bigelow, 1995.
Stranger than Fiction. Dir. Marc Forster, 2006.
Stranger than Paradise. Dir. Jim Jarmusch, 1984.
The Student of Prague. Dir. Paul Wegener, 1913.
Syriana. Dir. Stephan Gaghan, 2005.
Terminator Two: Judgment Day. Dir. James Cameron, 1991.
The Thirteenth Floor. Dir. Joseph Rusnak 1999.
Time Code. Dir. Mike Figgis, 2000.
Too Many Ways to Be Number One. Dir. Wai Ka-Fai, 1997.
A Trip to the Moon. Dir. Georges Méliès, 1902.
The Trouble with Harry. Dir. Alfred Hichcock, 1955.
The Truman Show. Dir. Peter Weir, 1998.
12 Monkeys. Dir. Terry Gilliam, 1995.
21 Grams. Dir. Alejandro González Iñárritu, 2003.
2001: A Space Odyssey. Dir. Stanley Kubrick, 1968.
The Vanishing Lady. Dir. Georges Méliès, 1896.
Vertigo. Dir. Alfred Hitchcock, 1958.
The Village. Dir. M. Night Shyamalan, 2004.
Waking Life. Dir. Richard Linklater, 2001.
Water for Maya. Dir. Stan Brakhage, 2000.
What Women Want. Dir. Nancy Myers, 2000.
Wild Strawberries. Dir. Ingmar Bergman, 1957.
The Wizard of Oz. Dir. Victor Fleming, 1939.
The Wrong Man. Dir. Alfred Hitchcock, 1956.

BIBLIOGRAPHY

Adams, P. Sitney. 2002. *Visionary Film: The American Avant-Garde 1943–2000*. 3rd ed. Oxford: Oxford University Press.
Altman, Rick. 2008. *A Theory of Narrative*. New York: Columbia University Press.
Andrew, J. Dudley. 1976. *The Major Film Theories*. Oxford: Oxford University Press.
Andrews, David. 2004. "An Oneiric Fugue: The Various Logics of *Mulholland Drive*." *Journal of Film and Video* 56(1): 25–40.
Bazin, Andre. 1967. *What Is Cinema?* Berkeley: University of California.
Biskind, Peter. 2004. *Down and Dirty Pictures: Miramax, Sundance, and the Rise of Independent Film*. New York: Simon and Schuster.
Bordwell, David, Janet Staiger, and Thompson, Kristin. 1985. *The Classical Hollywood Cinema: Film Style and Mode of Production to 1960*. London: Routledge.
Bordwell, David. 2002. "Film Futures." *SubStance* no. 97(31): 88–104.
———. 1985. *Narration in the Fiction Film*. Madison: University of Wisconsin.
———. 2004. "Neo-Structuralist Narratology and the Functions of Filmic Storytelling." In *Narrative Across Media: The Languages of Storytelling*, ed. Marie-Laure Ryan, 203–19. Lincoln: University of Nebraska.
———. 2006. *The Way Hollywood Tells It*. Berkeley: University of California.
Borges, Jose Luis. 1998. *Collected Fictions*. New York: Viking.
Branigan, Edward. 1992. *Narrative Comprehension and Film*. London: Routledge.
———. 2002. "Nearly True: Forking Plots, Forking Interpretations—A Response to David Bordwell's 'Film Futures.'" *SubStance* no. 97(31): 105–114.
———. 1984. *Point of View in the Cinema*. Berlin: Mouton.
Buckland, Warren. 2003. "A Sad, Bad Traffic Accident: The Televisual Prehistory of David Lynch's Film *Mulholland Drive*." *New Review of Film and Television Studies* 1(1): 131–47.
———, ed. 2009. *Puzzle Films: Complex Storytelling in Contemporary Cinema*. London: Wiley-Blackwell.
Cameron, Allan. 2006. "Contingency, Order, and the Modular Narrative." *Velvet Light Trap* 58 (Fall): 65–78.
Chion, Michel. 1994. *Audio-Vision: Sound on Screen*. Translated by Claudia Gorbman. New York: Columbia University Press.
Cook, Pam, and Mieke Bernink, eds. 1999. *The Cinema Book*. 2nd ed. London: British Film Institute.
Deleuze, Gilles. 1986. *Cinema 1: The Movement Image*. Translated by Hugh Habberjam and Barbara Tomlinson. Minneapolis: University of Minnesota Press.
del Mar Azcona, María. 2010. *The Multi-Protagonist Film*. Chichester: John Wiley and Sons, Ltd.

Denby, David. 2007. "The New Disorder: Adventures in Film Narrative." *New Yorker*. 5 March. <http://www.newyorker.com/arts/critics/atlarge/2007/03/05/070305crat_at-large_denby>.
Earle, William. 1968. "Revolt Against Realism in the Films." In *Film Theory and Criticism*, ed. Gerald Cohen and Marshall Mast, 32–42. Oxford: Oxford University Press.
Ebert, Roger. 2001. "Lost on Mulholland Drive." *Chicago Sun Times*. 16 April.
Eggington, William. 2001. "Reality Is Bleeding." *Configurations* 9: 207–29.
Elsaesser, Thomas. 1998. "Specularity and Engulfment." In *Contemporary Hollywood Cinema*, ed. Steve Neale and Murray Smith, 191–207. London: Routledge.
———. 2009. "The Mind-Game Film." In *Puzzle Films: Complex Storytelling in Contemporary Cinema*, ed. Warren Buckland, 13–41. London: Wiley-Blackwell.
———, ed. 1990. *Early Cinema: Space, Frame, Narrative*. London: British Film Institute.
Elsaesser, Thomas, and Warren Buckland. 2002. *Studying Contemporary American Film: A Guide to Movie Analysis*. London: Arnold.
Freud, Sigmund. 1937. *The Interpretation of Dreams*. G. Allen & Unwin.
———, 1955. "The Uncanny." In *The Standard Edition of the Complete Psychological Works of Sigmund Freud*, vol. 17, ed. James Strachey, 219–53. London: Hogarth.
Genette, Gerard. 1980. *Narrative Discourse Revisited*. Translated by Jane Lewin. Ithaca: Cornell University Press.
Gray, Richard. 2007. "Scientists Find Drug to Banish Bad Memories." *Telegraph* 1 July. <http://www.telegraph.co.uk/scienceandtechnology/science/sciencenews/3298988/Scientists-find-drug-to-banish-bad-memories.html>.
Grau, Christopher. 2006. "*Eternal Sunshine of the Spotless Mind* and the Morality of Memory." *The Journal of Aesthetics and Art Criticism* 64(1): 119–33.
Grodal, Torben Kraugh. 2000. "Subjectivity, Objectivity and Aesthetic Feelings in Film." In *Moving Images, Culture and the Mind*, ed. Ib Bindebjerg, 87–104. Luton: University of Luton Press.
Grusin, Jay David, and Richard Bolter. 2000. *Remediation: Understanding New Media*. Cambridge, MA: MIT Press.
Gunning, Tom. 1990. "The Cinema of Attractions: Early Film, Its Spectator, and the Avant-Garde." In *Early Cinema: Space, Frame, Narrative*, ed. Thomas Elsaesser, 56–62. London: British Film Institute.
Hampton, Howard. 2004. "True Romance." *Film Comment* XL(6): 30–34.
Hassler-Forest, Dan. 2006. "Multiple Narrative Structures." 28 July. <http://www.euronet.nl/users/mcbeijer/dan/home_burton.html>.
Hayles, Katherine N., and Nicholas Gessler. 2004. "The Slipstream of Mixed Reality: Unstable Ontologies and Semiotic Markers in the *Thirteenth Floor*, *Dark City*, and *Mulholland Drive*." *PMLA-Publications of the Modern Language Association of America* 119(3): 482–99.
Hudson, Jennifer. 2004. "'No Hay Banda, and Yet We Hear a Band': David Lynch's Reversal of Coherence in *Mulholland Drive*." *Journal of Film and Video* 56(1): 17–24.
Kaufman, Stanley. 2001. "Sense and Sensibility." *New Republic* 29 October.
Kawin, Bruce F. 1978. *Mindscreens: Bergman, Godard, and First-Person Film*. Princeton: Princeton University Press.
Kinder, Marsha. 2003. "Designing a Database Cinema." In *Cinema Features: The Cinematic Imaginary after Film*, ed. J. Weibel and P. Shaw, 346–53. Cambridge: MIT Press.
———. 2002. "Hot Spots, Avatars, and Narrative Fields Forever: Buñuel's Legacy for New Digital Media and Interactive Database Narrative." *Film Quarterly* 55(4): 2–15.
King, Geoff. 2002. *New Hollywood Cinema*. London: I.B. Tauris.

———. 2005. *American Independent Cinema.* London: I.B. Tauris.
———. 2003. "Spectacle, Narrative, and the Spectacular Hollywood Blockbuster." In *Movie Blockbusters*, ed. Julien Stringer, London: Routledge.
Kleinhans, Chuck. 1998. "Independent Features: Hopes and Dreams." In *The New American Cinema*, ed. Jon Lewis, 307–27. Durham: Duke University.
Kracauer, Siegfried. [1947] 2004. *From Caligari to Hitler.* Princeton: Princeton University Press.
Krzywinska, Tanya. 2005. "The Enigma of the Real: The Qualifications for Real Sex in Contemporary Art Cinema." In *The Spectacle of the Real: From Hollywood to Reality TV and Beyond*, ed. Geoff King, 223–34. Bristol: Intellect.
Lavik, Erland. 2006. "Narrative Structure in the *Sixth Sense*." *Velvet Light Trap* 58 (Fall): 55–64.
Lentzner, J.R., and D.R. Ross. 2005. "The Dreams That Blister Sleep: Latent Content and Cinematic Form in *Mulholland Drive*." *American Imago* 62(1): 101–23.
Lewis, Jon. 1998. *The New American Cinema.* Durham: Duke University Press.
Little, William G. 2005. "Surviving *Memento*." *Narrative* 13(1): 67–83.
Lopate, Philip. 2001. "*Mulholland Drive*." *Film Comment* 37(5): 44.
Maltby, Richard. 2003. *Hollywood Cinema.* 2nd ed. Oxford: Blackwell.
Manovich, Lev. 2001. *The Language of the New Media.* Cambridge, MA: MIT Press.
Martin-Jones, David. 2006. *Deleuze, Cinema and National Identity.* Edinburgh University Press.
McGowan, Todd. 2004. "Lost on *Mulholland Drive*: Navigating David Lynch's Panegyric to Hollywood." *Cinema Journal* 43(2): 67–89.
McMahan, Alison. 1999. "The Effect of Multiform Narrative on Subjectivity." *Screen* 40(2): 146–57.
Mottram, James. 2006. *The Sundance Kids: How the Mavericks Took Back Hollywood.* London: Faber and Faber.
Mulvey, Laura. 1989. *Visual and Other Pleasures. (Language, Discourse, Society).* London: Palgrave Macmillan.
Murray, Janet. 1997. *Hamlet on the Holodeck: The Future of Narrative in Cyberspace.* New York: The Free Press.
Neale, Steve and Murray Smith, eds. 1998. *Contemporary Hollywood Cinema.* London, New York: Routledge.
Nochimson, Martha P. 2002. "*Mulholland Drive*." *Film Quarterly* 56(1): 37–45.
Norris, Chris. 2004a. "Charlie Kaufman and Michel Gondry's Head Trip." *Film Comment* 40(2): 20–21.
———. 2004b. "Movie of the Moment: *Eternal Sunshine of the Spotless Mind*." *Film Comment* XL(2): 20–21.
Perlmutter, Ruth. 2005. "Memories, Dreams, Screens." *Quarterly Review of Film and Video* 22(2): 125–34.
Perren, Alisa. 2002. "Sex, Lies and Marketing: Miramax and the Development of the Quality Indie Blockbuster." *Film Quarterly* 55(2): 30–39.
Roberts, Adam. 2000. *Science Fiction.* London: Routledge.
Rushton, Richard. 2007. "Absorption and Theatricality in the Cinema: Some Thoughts on Narrative and Spectacle." *Screen* 48(1): 109–12.
———. 2004. "Early, Classical and Modern Cinema: Absorption and Theatricality." *Screen* 45(3): 226–44.
Ryan, Marie-Laure. 2004. "Metaleptic Machines." *Semiotica* 150(1/4): 439–69.
Schatz Thomas. 1993. "The New Hollywood." In *Film Theory Goes to the Movies*, ed. Jim Collins, Hillary Radner, and Ava Preacher Collins, 8–36. London: Routledge.

———, ed. 2004. *Hollywood: Critical Concepts in Media and Cultural Studies*, vol. 1. London: Routledge.
Scheunemann, Dietrich. 2003. "Activating the Differences: Expressionist Film and Early Weimar Cinema." In *Expressionist Film: New Perspectives*, ed. Dietrich Scheuenemann, 1–32. Rochester, UK: Camden House.
Sconce, Jeffrey. 2002. "Irony, Nihilism and the New American Smart Film." *Screen* 43(4): 349–69.
Simons, Jan. 2008. "Complex Narratives." *New Review of Film and Television Studies* 6(2): 111–26.
Smith, David. 2005. "*Eternal Sunshine of the Spotless Mind* and the Question of Transcendence." *The Journal of Religion and Film* 9(1). <http://www.unomaha.edu/jrf/Vol9No1/vol9no1.htm>.
Stam, Robert. 2000a. *Film Theory*. Malden: Blackwell.
———, ed. 2000b. *Film and Theory: An Anthology*. London: Blackwell.
Thomas, Peter. 2003. "Victimage and Violence: *Memento* and Trauma Theory." *Screen* 44(2): 200–07.
Todorov, Tzvetan. 1973. *The Fantastic: A Structural Approach to a Literary Genre*. Translated by Richard Howard. Cleveland: Case Western Reserve University.
Turbett, Dion. 2001. "'So Where Are You?': On Memento, Memory, and the Sincerity of Self-Deception." *CineAction* September: 2–10.
Wallace, David Foster. 1997. *A Supposedly Fun Thing I'll Never Do Again*. Boston: Back Bay Books.
Ward, Paul. 2005. "I Was Dreaming I Was Awake: Dreaming, Spectacle, and Reality in *Waking Life*." In *The Spectacle of the Real: From Hollywood to Reality TV and Beyond*, ed. Geoff King, Bristol: Intellect.
Weintraub, Bernard. 1997. "Average Hollywood Film Now Costs $60 Million." *New York Times* 5 March.
Wilson, George. 2006. "Transparency and Twist in Narrative Fiction Film." *The Journal of Aesthetics and Art Criticism* 64(1): 81–95.
Žižek, Slavoj. 2000. *The Art of the Ridiculous Sublime: On David Lynch's* Lost Highway. Seattle: Walter Simpson Center for the Humanities.

INDEX

A
actuality film, 39–40, 46, 49–50
Altman, Robert, 25–27
American New Wave. *See* New Hollywood
amnesia
    anterograde, 7
    Memento, 95–97, 102, 106
    Mulholland Drive and *Memento*, 10–12, 80
    subjective realism, 30, 55
anachronic structure, 117–18
analepsis, 11, 113
analytic editing, 22
Anderson, Paul Thomas
    episodic narratives, 24
    multi-strand narratives, 26
    smart films, 20
Andrews, David, 10, 74, 85–87, 92n3
Antonioni, Michelangelo, 16
Aronofsky, Darren, 4
art cinema, 35, 37n9, 37n11, 37b13, 110n5
    attractions, 46–47
    hybridity, 132–37
    Mulholland Drive, 68–69, 71–72
    multiform narrative, 6–8, 28
    New Hollywood, 14–16
    periods of narrative experimentation, 3
    smart films, 20–23
attractions, 8–10, 133
    blockbusters, 17–18
    early cinema, 39–47
    Mulholland Drive, 69–71
authenticity, 47
avant-garde, 8–9
    in Gunning, 41, 47–50
    See also attractions

B
Babel, 25, 27
Being John Malkovich, 60–61, 66

Bergman, Ingmar, 3, 16, 28, 63–66
Bolter, Richard, 41–42, 47, 50n2
Bordwell, David
    classical Hollywood, 35–36, 37n6, 37n12
    on forking-path narrative, 29
    narration and style, 21–24
    subjective realist narration, 53
    on three periods of narrative experimentation, 2–7
Borges, Jose Luis, 29, 37n12
boundaries
    diegetic, 113, 123–25
    ontological, 9, 11, 34, 127
Brakhage, Stan, 49, 66
Branigan, Edward
    deep internal focalization, 7
    on forking-path narratives, 29, 37n12
Brazil, 32–33
Buckland, Warren
    on classical Hollywood style, 22–23
    puzzle films, 5, 34–35, 36n5, 36n16
    spectacle, 43–44
Buñuel, Luis, 45, 46

C
Cabinet of Dr. Caligari, 8–9, 52, 68–73, 92, 92n1
Cameron, Allan, 117
Capra, Frank, 28, 110n5
causality, 23, 72
Chion, Michel, 131n3
cinema of attractions, 39–51, 92, 109, 130, 133
    avant-garde, 46–51
    early cinema, 8–10, 12
    German Expressionism, 70–71
classical Hollywood, 8, 9, 19, 21, 24, 37n9
    conventions of, 41–43
classical narration, 12, 29, 91

continuity style, 2, 8, 22, 40, 56–58, 70, 90, 110n7
Cook, Pam, 3
Coppola, Francis Ford, 3, 16, 41

D

defamiliarization, 8, 45
    Russian formalism, 46–50
    See also formalism
del Mar Azcona, María, 25
Deleuze, Gilles, 109n5, 110n7
Denby, David, 1, 4, 19, 134, 136
Deren, Maya, 31, 53–55

E

Earle, William, 48–50, 78, 91
Eggington, William, 125, 127
8½, 6, 8, 28, 30, 48, 52, 110n5
Elsaesser, Thomas
    on German Expressionist cinema, 71–72
    mind-game film, 34–35, 38n16
    narration, 22–23
    on New Hollywood, 15
    spectacle, 43–44
episodic narrative, 24, 26
Eternal Sunshine of the Spotless Mind, 1–13, 50, 55, 58, 63, 112–31, 132–37
    diegetic boundaries, 11
    smart film, 68
    as subjective realist multiform film, 9
experimental film, 49, 53–56, 75, 92n3
    in the 1960s, 16
    Maya Deren, 31
    Mulholland Drive, 10
    subjective realism, 36
    surrealism, 35

F

fantastic, 32, 38
    Eternal Sunshine of the Spotless Mind, 121–22
    Mulholland Drive, 59–63, 67n2, 67n4, 71–73, 85
    See also Todorov
Fellini, Federico, 3, 6, 16, 28, 110n5
Fight Club, 34, 60–62, 67n2, 101
film noir, 12, 66n1, 74, 83, 109
Fincher, David, 34, 66n1
focalization, 7, 125
Ford, John, 2
foregrounding, 48–49, 91, 109
forking-path, 5, 29–31, 37n12
formalism, 48, 142

formalist, 23, 47, 78
Forster, Mark, 4, 125
Fountain, The, 4, 50
fragmented narrative, 10–14, 134–35
    Eternal Sunshine of the Spotless Mind, 117, 129
    New Hollywood, 22–27, 29–34, 36
    Memento, 98–99, 103–5, 110n5, 111n7
    Mulholland Drive, 69, 75–77, 78–81, 94
    subjective realism, 54, 55, 58
Freud, Sigmund, 78–82, 93n4, 111n7

G

gaps (narrative), 34, 85
    causal, 127, 130
    cognitive, 23
    temporal, 12, 118
Genette, Gerard, 123
Gilliam, Terry, 31–33
Gondry, Michel, 113, 132
González Iñárritu, Alejandro, 1–2
Grodal, Torben Kraugh, 57–58
Groundhog Day, 28
Grusin, Jay David, 41–42, 47, 50n2
Gunning, Tom, 8, 39–46, 69–70

H

Hartley, Hal, 18, 26–27
Hassler-Forest, Dan, 26
Hayles, N. Katherine, 31–32
Hitchcock, Alfred, 3, 16, 124
Hollywood, 35–36, 36n5–6, 37n9, 37n11, 52, 56, 132–36
    attractions, 40–45
    Eternal Sunshine of the Spotless Mind, 104–6, 109n1, 110n5, 109n7, 112–14, 127, 130 *Mulholland Drive*, 69–71, 83–84, 88, 77–78, 90–91
    multiform narrative in, 31
    narrative experimentation in, 2–5
    New Hollywood, 14–24
    subjective realism in, 56–59
Hudson, Jennifer, 75–78, 84
hypermediacy, 4

I

illocutionary boundary, 123–24
immediacy, 2, 41–42, 47, 49, 50n2, 83
Inception, 2, 4, 9, 133, 136
Irreversible, 109n4
It's a Wonderful Life, 28, 110n5

J
Jarmusch, Jim, 18, 24, 26–27
Jonze, Spike, 20

K
Kaufman, Charlie, 19, 113, 115
Kawin, Bruce, 7, 53
Kieslowski, Krizysztof, 29
Kinder, Marsha, 4
King, Geoff, 22–27, 31, 37n7, 43–44
Korine, Harmony, 24
Kracauer, Siegfried, 70, 92n1
Krzywinska, Tanya, 45
Kubric, Stanley, 16
Kurosawa, Akira, 3, 6

L
Lacan, Jacques, 82–83
Lang, Fritz, 69–71
Last Year at Marienbad, 53
Lelouch, Claude, 16
Lentzner, Jay R., 78–85
Linklater, Richard, 20, 45, 133
Lynch, David, 4, 36n5, 55, 66n1, 69, 81–82, 86–87, 93n4

M
Martin-Jones, David, 104–06, 109n5–7
Magnolia, 26
McGowan, Todd, 82–85, 106
McMahan, Alison, 4, 8, 31–32, 38n13
Méliès, Georges, 8, 39–41, 46, 59, 71, 133
Memento, 4–5, 11–12, 19, 27, 30, 81, 94–111, 132–136
    as mind-game film, 34–36, 37n6
    as trance film, 53, 55, 67n2
Meshes of the Afternoon, 53–56
metadiegetic, 123–127
metalepsis, 113, 132–127
modernist, 6, 103
Montgomery, Robert, 3
Mulholland Drive, 4–13, 45, 53–63, 67n2, 68–93, 99–101, 107–08, 111n7, 132–135
    and *Memento*, 99–101
    multiform narrative, 30–32, 36n4–5
    multi-strand narrative, 27
    ontological fragmentation, 24
    subjective realist multiform film, 7
multi-strand narrative, 25–27, 134–35
    Brazil, 33
    Memento, 94
    Mulholland Drive, 10, 74
    and multiform narratives, 6, 31

Murnau, F.W., 70
Murray, Janet, 6–8, 28–32, 38n13, 55

N
Nakata, Hideo, 125
New Hollywood, 3, 7, 14–21, 36n5, 42–43, 133
Nietzsche, Frederic, 114–16
nihilism, 81, 93n4
Noe, Gaspar, 109n4
Nolan, Christopher, 2, 4, 67n4

O
ontological shifts, 3, 33–35, 59, 65, 78
ontological fragmentation, 94, 110n5
    Brazil, 32–33
    Mulholland Drive, 10, 80, 84
    subjective realism, 24–25, 30, 36

P
Paisa, 27
Perlmutter, Ruth
    on *Memento*, 106–07
    on *Mulholland Drive*, 75, 77–78, 84, 86, 92n3
    multiform narrative, 30–31
    subjective realism, 53–55
Preminger, Otto, 3
Prestige, The, 67n4

R
Ramis, Harold, 28
Rashomon, 6, 28, 30, 52, 140
realism, 56, 78, 83
    in Hollywood, 20–22
    and immediacy, 41–42
    Mulholland Drive, 88–89
    transparency and alternatives to, 46–50
    subjective, 53–56, 101–11
Resnais, Alain, 1–2, 10, 53
restricted narration, 58
    Cabinet of Dr. Caligari, 78
    Memento, 94–95, 101
    subjective realism, 58, 66n2
Ross, Donald R., 78–85
Rossellini, Roberto, 26
Rushton, Richard, 91
Ryan, Marie-Laure, 124

S
Scanner Darkly, A, 133
Sconce, Jeffrey
    art cinema, 3, 7, 20–21, 110n7

on smart films, 7, 20, 66n1, 108, 110n6, 110n7, 112, 133
Simons, Jan, 37n12
smart films, 12, 20–21, 110n7, 131, 133
Source Code, 4
spectacle, 9, 133
    blockbuster, 17–18
    in Hollywood, 41–45, 51n5
    See also attractions
Strange Days, 42, 55
Stranger then Fiction, 4, 125
Student of Prague, 46, 68, 70–72

T

Tarantino, Quentin, 1
Todorov, Tzvetan, 38n14
    Cabinet of Dr. Caligari, 73
    Eternal Sunshine of the Spotless Mind, 121
    on the fantastic, 59–63, 67n2
    Mulholland Drive, 85
Trumball, Douglas, 50n3
Turbett, Dion, 96, 100–04, 109n1
12 Monkeys, 31–32
Tykwer, Tom, 29

U

Un Chien Andalou, 41, 46, 49

uncanny
    Memento, 85, 89
    Mulholland Drive, 69–71
    science fiction, 38n14
    in Todorov, 61–65
    See also fantastic
unreliable narration
    Cabinet of Dr. Caligari, 72–73
    Memento, 5, 12, 98–107
    Mulholland Drive, 7, 86
    puzzle films, 34

V

Vertigo
    defamiliarization 48
    subjective realism, 56–57

W

Waking Life, 133
Wallace, David Foster, 69
Wegener, Paul, 46, 70
Weine, Robert, 6, 28, 71–72, 132
Welles, Orson, 2
Wilson, George, 5, 66n2

Z

Žižek, Slavoj, 55